HERE COMES ISHMAEL

Faisal Malick

bere comes ishmael

The KAIROS
MOMENT FOR The
MUSLIM PEOPLE

Belleville, Ontario, Canada

Here Comes Ishmael
Copyright © 2005 Faisal Malick

All Scripture quotations, unless otherwise specified, are from *The Holy Bible, King James Version.* Copyright © 1977, 1984, Thomas Nelson Inc., Publishers.

Scripture quotations marked NKJV are taken from the New King James Version. Copyright © 1979, 1980, 1982. Thomas Nelson Inc., Publishers.

Library and Archives Canada Cataloguing in Publication

Malick, Faisal, 1975-
     Here comes Ishmael / Faisal Malick.

ISBN 1-55306-943-9

     1. Christianity and other religions--Islam. 2.Islam--Relations--Christianity. 3. Malick, Faisal, 1975- 4. Christian converts from Islam--Biography. I.Title.

BT1170.M28 2005   261.2'7   C2005-902865-3

**For more information or
to order additional copies, please contact:**

Covenant of Life Media Inc.
P.O Box 43055
Mississauga, ON L5B 4A7
Tel :905-712-1453 • Fax::905-712-0445
E-mail: info@covenantoflife.org
Web site: www.covenantoflife.org

Guardian Books is an imprint of *Essence Publishing,* a Christian Book Publisher dedicated to furthering the work of Christ through the written word. For more information, contact:

20 Hanna Court, Belleville, Ontario, Canada K8P 5J2
Phone: 1-800-238-6376 • Fax: (613) 962-3055
E-mail: publishing@essencegroup.com • Internet: www.essencegroup.com

Printed in Canada
by

Guardian
B   O   O   K   S

Dedication

I dedicate this book to Ishmael and the 1.6 billion Muslim people he represents. You are not forgotten, but you are chosen for such a time as this. This is your season to embrace the truth about your origin and your end-time destiny, planned before creation. Your cry will be heard, and you will behold the Invisible in this hour.

I am sought of them that asked not for me; I am found of them that sought me not: I said Behold me, behold me, unto a nation that was not called by my name (Isaiah 65:1).

Acknowledgments

would like to thank my precious love and wife of substance, Sabina. You were the first to embrace the passion of this message and see the end from the beginning. You chose to stand in the gap for a misunderstood people and demonstrate the heart of Jesus. You have been an inspiration and encouragement to me throughout working on this book. I love you always. Without you even my destiny would be incomplete.

I would like to thank Pastor Stephen & Abby Oosthuyzen for embracing this message with a weeping heart of intercession and love while it was in its infancy. Thank you for helping with the editing of this book and looking beyond clay into our destiny.

I would like to thank those of you who remain anonymous in your prayer and support for this book. You know who you are and you are dear to my heart.

Table of Contents

Endorsements

I t is a joy to introduce to you, the reader, my spiritual son Faisal Malick. Faisal was radically saved on July 3, 1994. It was then that the Lord began to use him in the ministry. I believe that Faisal has a prophetic calling with a prophetic Message for this hour. Faisal has taken what the Lord has given him prophetically and written it in this book, *Here Comes Ishmael*. This book will inspire and challenge you concerning the last days and the move of God that is coming upon the Islamic nations of the world. *Here Comes Ishmael* is cutting edge and revolutionary and will not leave you the same. We are living in the greatest time of church history. Faisal, under the guidance of the Holy Spirit, has been empowered to capture some of the Father's heart for the end-time harvest. So, allow this book to shift you from *Chronos* to *Kairos*.

Dr. Stephen Oosthuyzen
Machseh Agencies International

The western mind, for the most part, does not comprehend the vast world of Muslim thought nor the history of

Islam. Faisal Malick has, with great skill, love and compassion, opened to us the inner workings of this world of thought and religion. *Here Comes Ishmael* is a must read! From the genesis of Islam to present Muslim thought, Faisal writes so that all can understand.

When you finish reading this book, I know that you will grasp God's love for all humanity and desire to connect these dear people with the Lord Jesus Christ.

This book has helped me set aside preconceived judgements and realize that Muslims are a people hungry for truth, love and understanding. This book is a most welcome revelation for our times.

Rev. Norm Maclaren
Vice President, Ministry
Crossroads Christian Communications

Faisal Malick has provided extraordinary prophetic, Biblical insight into the divine destiny of the Muslim people through Ishmael. This captivating work is a revelation that will activate intercession, compassion, and acceptance for the Islamic people as the time has now come for them to see Jesus and know the Father. Be transformed in your thinking and faith as you witness an unprecedented move of God on a global scale that is now beginning to unfold.

Len Zoeteman
Regular Guest – The Miracle Channel

Preface

The primary intent of this book is to define and clarify the season we are in and create awareness of the significance of Ishmael in our times. I pray that we see beyond the lenses of our limitations into the counsel of God.

This book is not just about God's mercy in reaching out to the Muslim world but the statement that God is making to Israel, the Church and the Nations of the earth in showing His mercy, love and compassion to the Muslim People. As you read this book I pray that you recognize the statement He is making to you and look into the fullness of His all encompassing purpose. This book is not just about the end times but more about the intent of God before the beginning of time. This is a message to the Muslim people but if we are not careful we may miss the message to us. For me this is not just a message I am sharing with you but a message that I am.

As you read the chapters ahead I believe you will recognize that God started in time what he already finished in eternity.

Kairos time is a moment when a portal is opened between time and eternity so that an event can take place in its fullness, as appointed by God, to forever change the destiny of man.

Chapter One

Ishmael and Islam

Today, 1.6 billion Muslims stand at center stage, while the world watches and wonders. Israel warns of terrorism, the Church is watching the clock, and the people of Islam are seeking a revolution. Simultaneously, a portal is opening between time and eternity over the Muslim world, making way for a *Kairos moment* to occur. Humanity is responding to the season we are living in; not just any season, but the Kairos moment for the Muslim people.

In Greek, time is divided into *Chronos* and *Kairos*. Chronos is chronological time, measured in seconds, minutes, days, and years. Kairos time is a moment when a portal is opened between time and eternity so that an event can take place in its fullness, as appointed by God, to forever change the destiny of man. Man knows time as Chronos and measures it. God knows time as Kairos and destines it. A Kairos moment opens the door to destiny, when that which has been hidden for ages is revealed. As the Church of Jesus Christ, we must discern Kairos moments so we can flow with God. In this chapter, we will discuss the Biblical origins of the Muslim people, the nature of their cry, and the heartbeat of God for this hour.

BIBLICAL ORIGIN OF THE MUSLIM PEOPLE

Mohammad, the prophet of Islam, was a direct descendent of Ishmael through his second son, Kedar. Mohammad received revelations from an angel whom he believed to be Gabriel. These revelations later became the book of the Muslims, known as the Qur'an. Muslims believe that Abraham took his firstborn Ishmael to the altar of sacrifice on the mount instead of Isaac to substantiate Ishmael as the seed through which the whole earth would be blessed. The Muslims also believe that Mohammad was the fulfillment of God's promise to Abraham and that Mohammad was the prophet like unto Moses. They consider the Bible to be changed and not entirely authentic. The nation of Islam comes forth from Ishmael's descendent Mohammad. So Islam's roots trace back to Ishmael. Later Ishmael married an Egyptian and his family vastly expanded through twelve sons, leading to a multitude of people. The Muslim people existed long before they embraced Islam. I have come to understand that God always looks at the root of an issue rather than merely the surface.

Muslims believe that Abraham took his firstborn Ishmael to the altar of sacrifice on the mount instead of Isaac

While Hagar was with child, the angel of the Lord found her in the wilderness and began to unveil God's plan:

And the angel of the LORD found her by a fountain of water in the wilderness, by the fountain in the way to Shur. And he said, Hagar, Sarai's maid,

*whence camest thou? and whither wilt thou go?
And she said, I flee from the face of my mistress
Sarai. And the angel of the* LORD *said unto her,
Return to thy mistress, and submit thyself under
her hands. And the angel of the* LORD *said unto
her, I will multiply thy seed exceedingly, that it shall
not be numbered for multitude* (Genesis 16:7-10).

GOD NAMED ISHMAEL BEFORE BIRTH

Ishmael was the first person to ever be named by God
before birth in all the earth. When something happens for the
first time in the Bible, it is very significant and sets a precedent.
It is called the law of first things. In
the entire Bible, there are only four
people that God named before they
were born through a divinely granted
appearance of an angel or of Himself.
There are others that God prophesied
about, but only four were named
before birth in this divine way. The
first was Ishmael, the second was
Isaac, the third was John the Baptist,
and the last was Jesus. (Genesis

*When something
happens for the
first time in the
Bible, it is very
significant and
sets a precedent.*

16:11, Genesis 17:19, Luke 1:13, Luke 1:31). The Church
knows the last three, but the first the Church has not seen.

And the angel of the LORD *said unto her, Behold,
thou art with child, and shalt bear a son, and shalt
call his name Ishmael; because the* LORD *hath
heard thy affliction* (Genesis 16:11).

Hagar went back to Sarai, as instructed by the angel of the
Lord, and Ishmael was born. When Ishmael was about thirteen

years old, God appeared to Abram and changed his name to Abraham (Genesis 17:5). God discussed his covenant with Abraham and promised to give him and Sarah a son. Abraham beseeched the Lord about Ishmael, and God responded:

> *And Abraham said unto God, O that Ishmael might live before thee! And God said, Sarah thy wife shall bear thee a son indeed; and thou shalt call his name Isaac: and I will establish my covenant with him for an everlasting covenant, and with his seed after him. And as for Ishmael, I have heard thee: Behold, I have blessed him, and will make him fruitful, and will multiply him exceedingly; twelve princes shall he beget, and I will make him a great nation. But my covenant will I establish with Isaac, which Sarah shall bear unto thee at this set time in the next year (Genesis 17:18-21).*

God blessed Ishmael and promised he would be exceedingly multiplied beyond number, with twelve princes, and would become a great nation. In Genesis 16:11, God named Ishmael before he was born, and in Genesis 17:20, God blessed Ishmael but established His covenant with Isaac, the promised seed. (We will discuss in detail why God blessed Ishmael in chapter seven, "The blessing of Ishmael.") Upon the weaning of Isaac, Sarah found Ishmael mocking Isaac and desired that the son of the bondwoman be cast out and not be an heir with her son, Isaac (Genesis 21:9). Abraham was grieved, like any father would be, and went to the Lord. God made it clear to him that in Isaac God's covenant would be established and in Isaac would his seed be called. As for Ishmael, he was to be cast out, but God confirmed again to Abraham that Ishmael would become a great nation. Ishmael, along with Hagar, was cast out of his father's house with no more than a little bread and water.

Wherefore she said unto Abraham, Cast out this bondwoman and her son: for the son of this bondwoman shall not be heir with my son, even with Isaac. And the thing was very grievous in Abraham's sight because of his son. And God said unto Abraham, Let it not be grievous in thy sight because of the lad, and because of thy bondwoman; in all that Sarah hath said unto thee, hearken unto her voice; for in Isaac shall thy seed be called. And also of the son of the bondwoman will I make a nation, because he is thy seed. And Abraham rose up early in the morning, and took bread, and a bottle of water, and gave it unto Hagar, putting it on her shoulder, and the child, and sent her away: and she departed, and wandered in the wilderness of Beersheba (Genesis 21:10-14).

THE WELL

Ishmael, around the age of fifteen, was cast out with Hagar into the wilderness. Let's see what happens:

And the water was spent in the bottle, and she cast the child under one of the shrubs. And she went, and sat her down over against him a good way off, as it were a bowshot: for she said, Let me not see the death of the child. And she sat over against him, and lift up her voice, and wept. And God heard the voice of the lad; and the angel of God called to Hagar out of heaven, and said unto her,

21

What aileth thee, Hagar? fear not; for God hath heard the voice of the lad where he is. Arise, lift up the lad, and hold him in thine hand; for I will make him a great nation. And God opened her eyes, and she saw a well of water; and she went, and filled the bottle with water, and gave the lad drink. And God was with the lad; and he grew, and dwelt in the wilderness, and became an archer. And he dwelt in the wilderness of Paran: and his mother took him a wife out of the land of Egypt (Genesis 21:15-21).

Ishmael wandered in the wilderness with Hagar and ran out of water. After being cast out of his father's house, he found himself dying in the wilderness under a shrub. Hagar could not look upon the pain of her dying son. In hopelessness, she left her son under a bush and walked away, crying out to God. She could not bear seeing her son die. All she could do was weep and cry out in her pain. All the while, the young boy himself lay under a bush dying. The young lad was not just physically dying, but his heart was already broken with rejection and his soul pierced with sorrow. In a moment, he went from being a son to merely a servant. "Who am I...the son of a patriarch, the father of many nations, or just the son of a servant?" His identity lay in conflict, and his image of a father was forever shattered. To make matters worse, at the door of death in the wilderness, his own mother left him to die alone. His condi-

> *In a moment, he went from being a son to merely a servant...His identity lay in conflict, and his image of a father was forever shattered*

22

tion was so bad that his mother could not watch him die. Ishmael was brought up all his life, learning about God from his father Abraham, but now where was that God? Had that God forsaken him and forgotten about him? The Bible says that God heard the voice of the lad and knew where he was (Genesis 21:17). Notice God did not hear the mother but the boy, in the very place he was: the place of death, pain, rejection, and thirst. The reason God heard the lad is because *Ishmael* means *God hears*. God knew the end from the beginning He named Ishmael

It took water to save his natural life, and it will take living water from the well of Jesus to save his spiritual life

before he was born because of the plan and destiny for his life. God heard his cry in the wilderness and opened the eyes of Hagar so that she could see a well of water and give Ishmael water to drink that he might live. Amazingly, the well was already there, but they could not see it.

Four thousand years later, the Muslim people are in a spiritual wilderness, with a cry that has only gotten deeper; dying of thirst, unable to see the well of their salvation. But God is going to hear the cry of Ishmael and open his eyes and show him the well of living water, which is Jesus, that he may drink and live. It took water to save his natural life, and it will take living water from the well of Jesus to save his spiritual life. The hour has come for the Muslim people to see Jesus and know the Father. We, as a Church, must discern the times we are living in and hear the sound of Heaven. We must intercede for the Muslims like a mother would for her dying child. Some of us have walked away from Ishmael, just like his own mother did, because the condition of Ishmael seems so hopeless in many ways; but we must yield to the Spirit of God and pray that God will awaken the cry that is in the hearts of the Muslim people and stir it so deep that it touches the heart of the Most High. We must pray that God will open the eyes of Ishmael. God will hear the cry of the Muslim people in this hour. God named Ishmael before he was born, in His wisdom, because one day he knew there would be 1.6 billion Muslims in a spiritual wilderness. Church, get ready—a whole generation of Muslims are going to come into the Kingdom. All of a sudden, 800 million to one billion Muslims are going to enter the Kingdom.

An earthquake hit on December 26, 2004, with its epicenter near Indonesia, the largest Muslim nation in the world, causing a tsunami that affected many other nations, resulting in hundreds of thousands of deaths. Folks, another earthquake of the glory of God is coming and the epicenter will be the Muslim people and will cause a tsunami of the Spirit to go into many other nations, bringing life. This spiritual earthquake will trigger the largest harvest the earth has ever seen. (We will discuss how all this shall be in chapter five.)

> *He will use another woman, the Church, to give living water to him today, out of the well of everlasting life.*

Intercession and prayer is the first step. Intercession is prayer that embraces the heart of God. The plans of the Spirit are birthed into this realm through prayer. We must not just pray but also be ready to move with God in this hour. God used a woman to give water to Ishmael to drink in the wilderness and He will use another woman, the Church, to give living water to him today, out of the well of everlasting life. Ishmael is thirsty for living water and hungry for fresh bread baked in the oven of God's Spirit. Jesus has always been a fisher of men. He desires to make us fishers of men so that we will be ready for this season. To really be fishers of men, it is necessary to understand the nature and cry of the Muslim heart.

THE CRY OF ISHMAEL

To understand the nature of the Muslim cry, we must once again go to the origins of this cry. The cry began when Ishmael was cast out of his father's house and left with no inheritance. For fifteen years, he grew up with the love of his father, Abraham, only to be cast out of his father's house, because the son of the bondwoman could not be heir with the son of the free woman (Genesis 21:10). Ishmael was cast out into the wilderness with a piece of bread and a bottle of water, the last thing his father ever gave him (Genesis 21:14). Ishmael must have looked to his mother for an explanation of what was happening, only to find her reminding him that he was the son of a servant and had no father. Ishmael waited in the wilderness, hoping his father would come looking for him and bring him bread and water again, but his father never came. The next time Ishmael ever saw his father was to bury him (Genesis 25:9). Ishmael didn't just bury Abraham but also buried his chance to ever be a son again. That burial signified the death of Ishmael's hope to ever be accepted or loved by a father again.

Identity is not just about who you are but whose you are.

At the core of the cry is a desire to be loved by a father and a need for an identity. Without a father, a son has no identity. Identity is not just about who you are but whose you are. If you don't know whose you are, you will never know who you are. If you don't know your identity, you define yourself by what you do. A son can be traced by his DNA to his father, but a servant is traced by his works. Ishmael was cast out and left with no father, identity, or inheritance. With no warning, Ishmael was abandoned, rejected, and fatherless. The right of every son is to receive an inheritance from his father. That right was taken away from Ishmael, leaving him with a seal of his fatherlessness. That cry lives on today in the Muslim people.

Centuries later, the children of Ishmael built a memorial around the cry of Ishmael and called it *Islam,* which means to submit to God much like a servant, rather than to have a relationship with him as a son. Islam filled the void of his heart, saying God is not a Father and has no Son. Islam became the face of God to Ishmael. Muslims still see themselves as servants or slaves submitting to God, hoping that, through their works, they can obtain acceptance and approval from God and avoid inevitable judgment. They seek to earn acceptance by God through works rather than grace. This is not just a moral code but the state of being of every Muslim. Regardless, the cry of Ishmael has never ceased but only gotten deeper with time.

> *Islam filled the void of his heart, saying God is not a Father and has no Son.*

Today, the Muslim people are still in this wilderness at the point of death. Once again, in this spiritual wilderness, there is a well that they cannot see. They have no father to give them bread nor water. At the same time, the Church is walking away from them, unable to watch them die. God is calling out to the Muslim people in this hour. He will hear their cry and open their eyes and show them the face of Jesus in the well of the living water of the glory of God. God will be their Father and give their hungry souls fresh bread from Heaven and thirsty hearts living water that they may live. God is going to manifest His glory among Ishmael and revive him in the presence of Jesus.

The Father is going to give an identity to the Muslim people in this hour. He will reveal to them the truth about their destiny hidden in the name of Ishmael. He will show them His covenant and give them an inheritance in Christ Jesus. He will never leave them nor forsake them. Rather, this archer, Ishmael, once born of the Spirit will become an arrow in the bow of God's hand shot right into the heart of the enemy that once blinded him.

He will reveal to them the truth about their destiny hidden in the name of Ishmael.

This is the Kairos moment for the Muslim people. Bright clouds of God's presence are forming and lightning flashes of His glory are moving over the Muslim world. There will be rain from Heaven and a great harvest of the Muslim people in this hour. The cry of Ishmael has come up before the throne of God, and the answer is on the way.

I can hear God speaking through the prophet Isaiah, saying:

> *I am sought of them that asked not for me; I am found of them that sought me not: I said, Behold me, behold me, unto a nation that was not called by my name* (Isaiah 65:1).

Behold, God is going to do a new thing, and it shall spring forth and make a way in the wilderness and rivers in the desert and we shall all see it (Isaiah 43:19). God will hear the cry of Ishmael in this hour. Will we hear the cry of God's heart in this hour? Will we respond to His cry?

Just when we get wise and think we know everything, God comes along and uses that which we think is not useful...

Chapter Two

Ishmael and the Church

God uses the foolish things of this world to confound the wise. Just when we get wise and think we know everything, God comes along and uses that which we think is not useful. It is amazing how the one we judge or give up on is the very same person that God will reach out to. I was one of those people myself.

Prior to Sunday, July 3,1994, at 12:45 p.m., I was a Muslim adamantly opposed to the Gospel of the Lord Jesus Christ. Born in Pakistan as a Sunni Muslim, I was brought up subconsciously to oppose the deity of Jesus. For years, after school every day, I would go straight to a special school to study the Qur'an. It was a required part of the Muslim life growing up. I was taught and believed Jesus to be no more than a prophet second to Mohammad. Like all Muslims, I believed that confessing or believing that Jesus was the Son of God was the worst unforgivable sin a Muslim could ever commit. I considered such confession to be blasphemy. I believed the Bible was changed and inaccurate.

As a Canadian businessman, I debated with many

Christians, attempting to convert them to Islam. When invited to church, my response would be "I don't go to church; I am a Muslim." One night, at a business convention in the United States with approximately 20,000 people, I was invited to a non-denominational Christian service on Sunday morning. I was promised a front-row seat that I could use after the service for the remainder of the business convention. I took the bait and showed up the next morning and found the first thirty to forty rows missing on the main floor in front of the stage. Puzzled, I went to a lady sitting in the front and asked why there was all this empty space in front of the stage. Her response was, "Something is going to happen here today." As I inquired further, her reply was "Don't worry, you will soon find out." My curiosity got the best of me, and I found a seat as close to the front as I could.

The earth could shake and the mountains could move, but there is nothing on this earth that could make me confess that your Jesus is the Son of God

A businessman got up to speak and declared that Jesus is the Son of God. I could not believe what he was saying, and I became angry. He went on to say that there was no name given among men by whom one could be saved except the name of Jesus and if any one rejected Him as Lord and did not believe on the Son of God, he would go to hell. I did not like that. Then he had the audacity to say, "There are only two books which claim to be the written Word of God—the Bible is and the other one is not." I knew he was talking about my book. I thought this man was deceived and decided to talk to him and straighten him out. Just about then, he gave an altar call. I wasn't sure what an altar was, or a call, but I was one of the first to run to the front, thinking this would be my chance to speak to this man. Thousands rushed to the front from all directions to receive Jesus as their Savior. I thought about leaving but couldn't and got stuck to the stage. Then this man proceeded to lead us in a prayer that began with "Jesus is the Son of God." I said "No way," and confessed my *Kalma* as a Muslim instead. On my way back to my seat, two friends tried to hug and congratulate me for going to the front to give my heart to Jesus. I asked if they were crazy and declared, "I am a Muslim; don't ever call me a Christian. The earth could shake and the mountains could move, but there is nothing on this earth that could ever make me confess that your Jesus is the Son of God."

In a few months, I went to another convention and went to the Sunday service to save a seat and heard a businessman get up to preach Jesus as Lord. An altar call was given, and a second time I ran to the front; thousands followed. Immediately, I realized those people were being evangelized into Christianity through the preaching of the Gospel. I made a determined decision at this altar that I would learn what those people do and do it better than them and convert Christians in particular to Islam. After making that decision, I began to proceed with my plans.

> *I made a determined decision at this altar that I would learn what those people do and do it better than them and convert Christians in particular to Islam*

A few months later, I went to a third business convention in the United States. I now understood Christian terminology and understood that when someone said they were born again, they had received Jesus as their personal Lord and Savior and became a child of God. I got myself a front seat. Someone got up and preached that one can become a child of God and know God as Father through Jesus Christ, His only begotten Son. He went on to say that Jesus is the only way, the truth, and the life. After his preaching, he asked us all to stand, so we all stood. Then he began to give an altar call. (This time I did not go and knew I did not need to.)

As I was standing there, suddenly the living God showed up. At once, God's presence permeated right through me, encircled and arrested me. Engulfed in His Holy presence, immediately I knew I stood before God. My entire existence faded; He was all that mattered. When God shows up, you will know it with every fiber of your being: spirit, soul, and body. I had many questions going through my mind, but the longer I stood before Him, my questions disappeared. I asked Him one sincere question, saying, "God, what are You doing here? I thought these were the bad guys [referring to the Christians]?" I could not understand why God would manifest Himself among a people who were blaspheming God by worshiping Jesus as the Son of God. The answer came, and I heard these words, "No, *these are my children.*" Again, "No, *these are my children,*" and a third time, "No, *these are my children.*" His words echoed right through me, and immediately the veil was removed from my eyes. I knew nothing else but this reality that **Jesus is the Son of God!** This same Jesus whom I fervently denied I now could not live without. I went forward and confessed with my own mouth that Jesus is the Son of God, He was born of a virgin, died on the cross, and

> *Engulfed in His Holy presence, immediately I knew I stood before God. My entire existence faded. He was all that mattered.*

34

shed His blood for me, and I believed in my heart that God raised Him from the dead on the third day. My prayer was, "Father, take away my stony heart and give me a new heart of flesh. Jesus, come into my heart, be my Lord, that I may love the Father even as Thee." I became a new creation on that Sunday, July 3, 1994, at 12:45 p.m.

I knew by revelation that Jesus is the Son of God. In Matthew 16:15-17, Jesus turned and asked His disciples, *"But whom say ye that I am?"* Peter answered and said, *"Thou art the Christ, the Son of the living God."* Jesus responded and said to him, *"Flesh and blood hath not revealed it unto thee, but My Father which is in heaven."* Peter knew by revelation knowledge that Jesus really was the Christ and the Son of the living God. The Father revealed it to him by the Holy Spirit. That is the best way I can explain what happened to me. I thank God for reaching out to me and showing me His loving kindness. Maybe while you are reading this book, you too have a loved one that is blinded to the reality of Jesus. Let this be an encouragement to your faith that God can reach out to your loved one as well.

ISHMAEL AND SAUL

As we study Saul and the early church, let us allow the Holy Spirit to paint a prophetic picture of Ishmael and today's church.

The early Church was in the midst of great persecution. The foremost enemy of the Gospel was Saul, who even consented to the death of Stephen, causing believers in Christ to be scattered abroad all over Judea and Samaria (Acts 8:1). He was an educated Hebrew, an Israelite from the tribe of Benjamin, and, as far as the law was concerned, he was a Pharisee (Philippians 3:5). This Saul ravaged the early church with violence and cruelty. He went into every house and dragged men and women and put them in prison for their belief in the Lord Jesus Christ (Acts 8:3). To complicate things further, he went to the high priest of that day with murderous intentions and threats against the disciples. He obtained warrants to go into the synagogues, arrest believers, and bring them back to Jerusalem for imprisonment. He was hostile and determined to put an end to what he considered blasphemy against God:

> *And Saul, yet breathing out threatenings and slaughter against the disciples of the Lord, went unto the high priest, And desired of him letters to Damascus to the synagogues, that if he found any of this way, whether they were men or women, he might bring them bound unto Jerusalem* (Acts 9:1-2).

Saul assumed his actions of violence toward the Church were of God. Yet he was, in reality, resisting the Son of God. He justified his attitude of pride and hatred for the disciples through the law that he was so well acquainted with. He knew the Scriptures but not the **One** that was spoken of in the Scriptures. He was driven by a zeal for God yet was without knowledge of the truth. The Lord he thought he was serving, in reality, he was opposing. Saul changed in a sudden encounter with the Lord Jesus on the road to Damascus. He saw the light of the glory of God and fell to the earth from which man was made, humbled by the majesty of God. His self-will was broken, his pride shattered, his zeal consumed, and his mind subdued by the glory of Jesus Christ. While on the ground, Saul heard the voice of the Master:

> *Suddenly there shined round about him a light from heaven: And he fell to the earth, and heard a voice saying unto him, Saul, Saul, why persecutest*

thou me? And he said, Who art thou, Lord? And the Lord said, I am Jesus whom thou persecutest: it is hard for thee to kick against the pricks. And he trembling and astonished said, Lord, what wilt thou have me to do? And the Lord said unto him, Arise, and go into the city, and it shall be told thee what thou must do. And the men which journeyed with him stood speechless, hearing a voice, but seeing no man. And Saul arose from the earth; and when his eyes were opened, he saw no man: but they led him by the hand, and brought him into Damascus. And he was three days without sight, and neither did eat nor drink (Acts 9:3-9).

At the feet of Jesus, Saul the murderer became Paul the martyr. His zeal for the law was consumed with a passion for Jesus Christ. God had great purpose hidden in Paul, beyond what man could ever see. Paul was a chosen vessel for the Master's use in bearing the name of Jesus before Gentiles, kings, and all of Israel. Paul suffered much for the Gospel's sake but considered it a privilege to share the mysteries of the Gospel to a Gentile world.

Much of the Church today is afraid of Ishmael as the early Church was afraid of Saul. Ishmael is wreaking havoc around the world and is the cause of much persecution to the Church. Television and the media are constantly bombarding us with stories of war, terrorism, and violence surrounding the Muslim world. In reality, not all Muslims are violent or terrorists, but there are certain elements of terrorism in Islam that we will discuss later in the book. Regardless, terrorism and Islam are synonyms in the world today. Saul was the foremost terrorist of his day. He threw stones instead of bombs, but his intent at heart was to destroy those he perceived to be the enemies of God. There are some among Ishmael doing the same today.

Muslims believe they are serving God in opposing the deity of Jesus Christ. Let me give you an example. The Dome of the Rock dominates the skyline of Jerusalem and, from the Muslim point of view, it is a symbol of Islam to the world. It is the third-most-holy site to Muslims and the earliest monument celebrated by Muslims. They recognize it to be Mount Moriah, where Abraham offered Ishmael instead of Isaac. Second, they believe the prophet of Islam ascended to Heaven from this rock in a night journey. This Dome is also symbol of superiority before God above Christians and Jews. Muslims believe they have the final and last revelation from God and sincerely oppose all others. To represent this attitude, the inscriptions and writings on the Dome of the Rock are passages from the Qur'an opposing the deity of Jesus, to let the world know that Jesus is not the Son of God. Muslims are sincere about their zeal for God, yet without knowledge of the truth. Just as Saul was the most unlikely candidate for the Kingdom, most would consider Ishmael to be the last to realize that Jesus is the Son of God.

Just as Saul was the most unlikely candidate for the Kingdom, most would consider Ishmael to be the last to realize that Jesus is the Son of God.

Like Saul, Ishmael is about to have a head-on collision with the glory of the Lord Jesus Christ. The Father is about to show the face of Jesus to the Muslim people of the world. The Jesus he has opposed will become his Lord. (We will discuss how this shall be in chapter five.) God has great purpose hidden in the Muslim people. Ishmael will be a chosen vessel in the hands of God. After God opens the eyes of Ishmael, He will use him for the purposes of the Kingdom. There is destiny camouflaged in the Muslim people yet to be seen. We see them like Saul, but God sees them like Paul for such a time as this.

God is going to use the conversion of Ishmael to stir up the Church as He used the conversion of Saul to stir up the Church in the midst of persecution. The early Church was afraid of Saul in the hour of persecution and all that heard of his conversion were amazed. Likewise today, the Church will be amazed at the mass conversion of Ishmael. Even his own brethren in the flesh will be provoked to kill him, but Ishmael is not afraid of death or his enemies. Rather, this archer, once born of the Spirit, will be an arrow in the bow of God's hand shot into the heart of the enemy (Satan) who once blinded him. Jesus knows how to turn a murderer into a martyr for the Kingdom. There will be a holy fear of God and comfort of the Holy Ghost in the Church. The conversion of Ishmael will edify the Church and multiply the Church exceedingly. It will bring an awe and reverential fear of God to the Church. That is exactly what happened to the early Church (Acts 9:31).

Second, God will use Ishmael to provoke the Church into a passion for Jesus. What the Church has forsaken Ishmael will embrace. Ishmael has been in the desert, thirsty and hungry for fresh bread and living water. Once his eyes are opened, he will not hold back from the cause of Christ. Ishmael has been trained in the wilderness and is not afraid of his enemies. He will be grateful for Jesus the Messiah and count no cost too great to know the Master. Saul, the enemy of the Gospel, was transformed into Paul, the Apostle, who wrote these words inspired by the Holy Spirit:

> *God will use Ishmael to provoke the Church into a passion for Jesus. What the Church has forsaken Ishmael will embrace.*

I count all things but loss for the excellency of the knowledge of Christ Jesus my Lord: for whom I have suffered the loss of all things, and do count them but dung, that I may win Christ, And be found in him, not having mine own righteousness, which is of the law, but that which is through the faith of Christ, the righteousness which is of God by faith: That I may know him, and the power of his resurrection, and the fellowship of his sufferings, being made conformable unto his death (Philippians 3:8-10).

The passion that Ishmael will have for Jesus will be endless. His love for Jesus will be no secret and will be contagious to the Church. His passion for Jesus will provoke the Church to step out of complacency and familiarity of religion. Being provoked pricks our lukewarm hearts and allows us to look beyond false finish lines and comfort zones into the face of God. God provokes us to catch our attention and adjust our focus so that we may fix our eyes upon Jesus and what God is doing. It is important that we see the invisible and believe for the impossible. Ishmael will embrace his destiny and pursue the righteousness which is of God, through faith, rather the righteousness of man, through works. His true identity in Christ will emerge. His zeal will be replaced by the power of God. The supernatural intervention of God among the Muslim people is very significant to the age we are living in. God has already begun this work, and we are hearing of stories around the world of dynamic con-

> *Being provoked pricks our lukewarm hearts and allows us to look beyond false finish lines and comfort zones into the face of God.*

versions of Muslims to Christ. We are about to see this happen to an entire generation of Muslims.

THE CHURCH AND ANANIAS

Jesus appeared to Ananias in a vision concerning Saul's conversion:

> *And there was a certain disciple at Damascus, named Ananias; and to him said the Lord in a vision, Ananias. And he said, Behold, I am here, Lord. And the Lord said unto him, Arise, and go into the street which is called Straight, and enquire in the house of Judas for one called Saul, of Tarsus: for, behold, he prayeth, And hath seen in a vision a man named Ananias coming in, and putting his hand on him, that he might receive his sight. Then Ananias answered, Lord, I have heard by many of this man, how much evil he hath done to thy saints at Jerusalem: And here he hath authority from the chief priests to bind all that call on thy name. But the Lord said unto him, Go thy way: for he is a chosen vessel unto me, to bear my name before the Gentiles, and kings, and the children of Israel: For I will show him how great things he must suffer for my name's sake (Acts 9:10-16).*

Jesus told Ananias, in a vision, to go and pray for Saul of Tarsus so he could receive his sight back. Ananias was astonished at the Lord's instructions and tried to convince the Lord of how evil Saul was. He sincerely reasoned with Jesus about the nuisance Saul had been to the believers in Christ. It was hard for Ananias to wrap his mind around the fact that God was asking him to go and pray for such a person.

Jesus commanded Ananias to go and carry out his assignment while graciously revealing to him the greater purpose of God in choosing Saul. Jesus allowed Ananias to see Saul through God's eyes by telling him how Saul would bear the name of Jesus before Gentiles, kings, and all Israel for the glory of God.

I believe the Church is in a similar place concerning the Muslim people. The reputation of Ishmael in the world is one of war, violence, and terrorism. The Church has only seen Ishmael as Abraham's mistake and a work of the flesh that we have to live with. Like Ananias, God is opening our eyes to see Ishmael in light of His purpose. The Lord is not willing that any perish and is unveiling the destiny of the Muslim people.

God is opening our eyes to see Ishmael in light of His purpose.

You may be reading this today and wondering how this could be, or Jesus may be speaking to you about your role in this Kairos moment for the Muslim people. You may have a burden for them and the need to be in your prayer closet interceding for them as a whole or even individually. It is important to know your role in this marvelous harvest. I believe that, as we continue through the ninth chapter of the book of Acts, we will find the answer to our function as the Church in this hour:

> And Ananias went his way, and entered into the house; and putting his hands on him said, Brother Saul, the Lord, even Jesus, that appeared unto thee in the way as thou camest, hath sent me, that thou mightest receive thy sight, and be filled with the Holy Ghost. And immediately there fell from his eyes as it had been scales: and he received sight

forthwith, and arose, and was baptized. And when he had received meat, he was strengthened (Acts 9:17-19).

Obedience is the first step, and the key to it all is to hear what the Spirit is saying and obey. The Holy Spirit will challenge our limitations with revelation in the Word of God and illuminate our understanding. Ananias carried out the instructions of the Lord and saw the results; the Church must do the same.

All nations are made of one blood and redeemed through the blood of one, Jesus Christ...

Chapter Three

Ishmael and Israel

The almighty God of Heaven and Earth is not a respecter of persons and loves all. God is love and the Father of lights. All nations are made of one blood and redeemed through the blood of one, Jesus Christ. However not all in the earth have become partakers of this redemption. God in the New Testament recognizes humanity in three groups of people: the Jews, the Gentiles (nations), and the Church:

> *Give none offence, neither to the Jews, nor to the Gentiles, nor to the church of God* (1 Corinthians 10:32).

He loves all of them and has a plan for all of them. Our Heavenly Father wills that none should perish and that all would come to salvation in Christ Jesus. Going back to the days of Noah, we see that, after the flood, Noah replenished the earth (Genesis 9). Noah gave birth to the nations, and from the nations, God separated unto Himself a people through Abraham, Isaac, and Jacob known as the Jews. God had made a covenant with Abraham:

Now the LORD had said unto Abram, Get thee out of thy country, and from thy kindred, and from thy father's house, unto a land that I will shew thee: And I will make of thee a great nation, and I will bless thee, and make thy name great; and thou shalt be a blessing: And I will bless them that bless thee, and curse him that curseth thee: and in thee shall all families of the earth be blessed (Genesis 12:1-3).

Abraham had no children and God promised he would have seed to fulfill the promise of God. Right from the beginning, God's intention in separating a Jewish people was to eventually bless the families of the earth. Gods long-term plan was for the Gentiles to come into the Kingdom in due order. *"In Isaac shall thy seed be called"* (Genesis 21:12) was the promise of God to Abraham and likewise to Isaac concerning Jacob. Then Jacob became Israel, the father of the twelve tribes of Israel.

In essence, God separated a people unto Himself so that, through their seed, He could bless the rest of the peoples of the earth. This, for centuries, left two groups of people on the earth: Jews and Gentiles. The Jews were blessed and partakers of God's covenant. The Gentile people were strangers to the covenants and promises of Israel, without God in the earth (Ephesians 2:12).

Israel went after gods who were not God, and likewise, God will go after them who are no people.

But God took away that middle wall of partition between Jew and Gentile, on the cross, allowing all who would believe on Jesus to become one Body in Christ Jesus. This group is made of all mankind: Jews and Gentiles (nations) alike, transformed into a new creature in Christ Jesus who is Messiah to the Jew, Savior to the world, and Lord to the Church. We are stones fitly joined together into one Body of the Lord Jesus Christ.

To the Jewish people, the most noticeable of the Gentiles is Ishmael, because he was cast out of Abraham's house and left with no inheritance and no chance to ever be an heir. He was left to remain the son of a servant named Hagar:

> *Wherefore she said unto Abraham, Cast out this bondwoman and her son: for the son of this bondwoman shall not be heir with my son, even with Isaac* (Genesis 21:10).

Israel takes pride in the very fact that God separated unto Himself Abraham from the nations, Isaac from Ishmael, and Jacob from Esau. The Jewish people are secure in knowing that God, by election, chose Isaac, the father of Jacob (Israel), over Ishmael, the son of the bondwoman. Ishmael was born of the flesh and, upon mocking Isaac, was cast out from the law, the promises, and the covenants of Israel. The Muslims today surround Israel and yet are considered no people, from a covenant perspective, to the Jewish people.

ISRAEL MUST BE PROVOKED TO JEALOUSY AND ANGER

God spoke by the prophet Moses concerning Israel:

> *But I say, Did not Israel know? First Moses saith, I will provoke you to jealousy by them that are no people, and by a foolish nation I will anger you* (Romans 10:19, Deuteronomy 32:21).

Long ago, Israel provoked God to jealousy by going after strange gods. Israel provoked God to anger by committing abominations unto Him, such as sacrificing unto idols. Israel went after gods who were not God, and likewise, God will go after them who are no people. Israel took foolish idols to anger God; likewise God will take a foolish nation to anger Israel. The Bible says *"no people,"* meaning a people of no covenant with God, strangers to the promises of God made to Israel. Romans 11:11 says that, through the salvation of the Gentiles, Israel is provoked to jealousy.

There is no greater Gentile to provoke Israel to jealousy than Ishmael, nor a more foolish nation to anger Israel than Islam. The Muslims are the least likely people in the eyes of Israel to be worthy of salvation and God's outstretched hand of goodness. As far as Israel is concerned, Ishmael is still mocking them in war, violence, and terrorism. Ishmael is the last person Israel expects God would reach out to. The law of God they so diligently serve cast out Ishmael with no inheritance, making him a stranger to the covenants of Israel. The law did cast him out, but the grace of Jesus Christ will bring him in. Ishmael was cast out for Isaac's sake, but God will bring him into the Kingdom for Israel's sake. The salvation of the Muslim people will provoke Israel to jealousy for the Messiah. When Israel sees the outstretched arm of God, which brought them out of Egypt, reach out and bring Ishmael out of the wilderness, into the city of God, Israel will be provoked to jealousy for the Messiah. When God quenches the thirst of Ishmael in the waters of everlasting life, Israel will long for the water that once was hewn out of the rock.

The glory of God revealed to the Muslim people will anger

Ishmael was cast out for Isaac's sake, but God will bring him into the Kingdom for Israel's sake.

Israel to seek the face of God. When Israel sees the Shekinah glory they rejected on the mount manifested among the Muslim people, they will be angered and seek the face of God.

IMAGINE ISHMAEL SAYING TO ISRAEL:

- I was born of the bondwoman and **the law cast me out,** but the grace of Jesus Christ has brought me in.
- I was deprived of the **blessing of Abraham,** but now, in Christ Jesus, I am the seed of Abraham and an heir according to the promise (Galatians 3:29).
- I grew up without a **father** in the wilderness, but now **your** God is my Father.
- I had no **inheritance** from my father, but now I have obtained an inheritance that you have not, because I am a son and **heir** of God through Christ.
- I have received the promise of the Holy Spirit as a deposit of my inheritance (Ephesians 1:13-14).
- The new covenant that was promised to you in the prophets I now walk in (Jeremiah 31:33).
- I received the righteousness of God without the law through faith (Romans 3:21-28).
- I have tasted and seen that the Lord is good.
- To you were committed the oracles of God but unto me the Spirit of God (Romans 2:29).
- To you was the glory on the mount veiled in the face of Moses, but to me the exceeding glory is unveiled in the face of Jesus (2 Corinthians 3:7-9).
- To you was given the ministration of condemnation but unto me the ministration of righteousness (2 Corinthians 3:9).

51

Oh, how God uses the foolish things of this world to confound the wise (1 Corinthians 1:27). The destiny of the Muslim people has long been hidden in Ishmael. God named him before birth, knowing one day he would be an instrument in the hand of God to provoke Israel to jealousy and anger.

Israel was in the wilderness for forty years before entering the promised land, but Ishmael has been in the wilderness for 4,000 years, waiting to enter the promised land of God's salvation.

The Mystery of Israel's Sight

For I would not, brethren, that ye should be ignorant of this mystery, lest ye should be wise in your own conceits; that blindness in part is happened to Israel, until the fulness of the Gentiles be come in (Romans 11:25).

> *God named him before birth, knowing one day he would be an instrument in the hand of God to provke Israel to jealousy and anger.*

Let us be careful not to be high minded about our salvation and pointing fingers at the Jews for their stubbornness or their being cast away for a season. We are only partakers of the mercy of God. Let us not be wise in our own conceits and become ignorant of the mystery that blindness in part has happened to Israel, until the fullness of the Gentile population comes in.

Israel has been blinded by God for a season and only until the fullness of the Gentiles comes into the Kingdom. The rest of the world has been blinded by the god (Satan) of this world (2 Corinthians 4:4).

The fullness of the Gentiles must come in before the scales will fall off the eyes of Israel so they can see the Messiah. Nearly 42 percent of the world's Gentile population is Muslim. There can be no fullness of the Gentiles without the Muslim people. I believe the Muslim people are the epicenter for a Holy Ghost earthquake that will cause a tsunami of the glory of God to go into the nations of the world. They have a vital role in this end-time harvest. The Muslim harvest will trigger the harvest of other nations. When the world sees God the Father's outstretched arm to the Muslim people, the rest of the unbelieving world will long to know the Father. God is love, and whenever His love is displayed, the hungry human heart melts before Him.

By provoking Israel to jealousy, God will get their attention; by provoking Israel to anger, God will get their passion...

God will use Ishmael and the rest of the Gentiles to remove the scales from the eyes of the Jewish people. The fullness of the Gentiles must come in to remove the scales from the eyes of Israel so they can recognize the Messiah.

By provoking Israel to jealousy, God will get their attention; by provoking Israel to anger, God will get their passion to seek after the Messiah. By bringing in the fullness of the Gentiles, God will remove the scales from the eyes of Israel so they can see the Messiah. Once Israel recognizes the Messiah, they will seek after Him even in the midst of affliction (Hosea 5:15). When their eyes are open, they will finally say, *"Blessed is He that cometh in the name of the Lord"* (Matthew 23:39). The return of the Lord is nigh.

THE LAST SHALL BE FIRST AND THE FIRST LAST

The Jews were first, and they have become last, and the Gentiles were last and have become first. The fall of the Jews is the salvation of the Gentiles, and the salvation of the Gentiles is the provoking of the Jews unto jealousy (Romans 11:11). The casting-away of the Jews is the reconciling of the world, and the receiving of them is life from the dead (Romans 11:15). The unbelief of the Jews is the obtaining of mercy of the Gentiles, and the mercy of the Gentiles is the obtaining of mercy of Israel (Romans 11:30-31). The severity of God toward Israel is the goodness of God toward the Gentiles (Romans 11:22). The blindness of the Jews is the fullness of the Gentiles coming in, and the fullness of the Gentiles is sight to Israel (Romans 11:25).

The bringing of Israel home from around the world will show the world that He is God. But the bringing of Ishmael home from the wilderness will show the Jews that Jesus is the Messiah. When God hears the cry of Ishmael, He will open the eyes of the Muslims and show them the face of Jesus Christ. When Israel says, *"Blessed is He that cometh in the name of the Lord"* (Matthew 23:39), the Lord Jesus shall return.

The problem governments face is the inability to identify potential future terrorists, because they are living simple lives and carrying on business as usual, until suddenly one moment they answer the call to holy war...

Chapter Four

Ishmael and Esau

There is an element of terrorism and war within the Muslim world today. This particular element is at the center of the world's stage. With all the television and media coverage, it is a difficult subject to ignore. Some countries are concerned about the rapid growth of Muslim populations within their borders for fear of potential Islamic fundamentalism. Dormant cells of fundamentalists are scattered across the western world, leaving much concern for a new enemy from within. The problem governments face is the inability to identify potential future terrorists, because they are living simple lives and carrying on business as usual, until suddenly one moment they answer the call to holy war. This makes it very difficult, because governments do not want to point fingers at the Muslim world at large and cause unnecessary upheaval. Yet there are many unanswered questions about the origins and extent of terrorism and violence in the Muslim world. In this chapter, I would like to share with you Biblical insight into such matters.

First, let us look at Esau, then we will talk about Ishmael and Esau and their connection to terrorism. Rebekah, Isaac's wife, was the mother of Esau and Jacob. She was pregnant with twins, and even before birth, these two nations struggled with one another in her womb. She went to ask the Lord about all this:

> *And the children struggled together within her; and she said, If it be so, why am I thus? And she went to enquire of the LORD. And the LORD said unto her, Two nations are in thy womb, and two manner of people shall be separated from thy bowels; and the one people shall be stronger than the other people; and the elder shall serve the younger* (Genesis 25:22-23).

Esau was to serve the younger, though contrary to normal tradition and culture. Two very differently natured people were separated from her womb and Esau became stronger than Jacob. Today, the people of Esau are stronger than the people of Jacob.

> *And the boys grew: and Esau was a cunning hunter, a man of the field; and Jacob was a plain man, dwelling in tents* (Genesis 25:27).

Esau grew up a skilled hunter, and he was a man of the wild. Esau was a strong man, and his descendants would be much like him.

ESAU DESPISES HIS BIRTHRIGHT

Esau sold his birthright for a bowl of soup. He came in tired from the field and begged Jacob for some "red pottage" (Genesis 25:30). Esau despised his birthright and sold it for a bowl of lentils and bread (Genesis 25:31-34).

JACOB STEALS ESAU'S BLESSING

Isaac was getting old, and his eyes were dim. He wanted to pass on the blessing of Abraham to his eldest son, Esau, before he died. So Isaac sent him out to hunt some game and prepare food for him so he could eat it and bless Esau:

Now therefore, please take your weapons, your quiver and your bow, and go out to the field and hunt game for me. And make me savory food, such as I love, and bring it to me that I may eat, that my soul may bless you before I die (Genesis 27:3-4 NKJV).

Rebekah overheard Isaac and told Jacob to fetch some meat, so that she could make the food for Isaac, in order that Jacob could receive the blessing from Isaac instead of Esau. She devised a plan to clothe Jacob with Esau's clothes so that he would smell like Esau. She also covered his arms and neck with goat hair so that Jacob would seem as hairy as Esau (Genesis 27:14,17). The plan worked, and Isaac blessed Jacob and gave him the blessing of Abraham. Isaac blessed Jacob and the blessing is recorded in two parts in the Bible:

Therefore God give thee of the dew of heaven, and the fatness of the earth, and plenty of corn and wine: Let people serve thee, and nations bow down to thee: be lord over thy brethren, and let thy mother's sons bow down to thee: cursed be every one that curseth thee, and blessed be he that blesseth thee (Genesis 27:28-29).

And God Almighty bless thee, and make thee fruitful, and multiply thee, that thou mayest be a multitude of people; And give thee the blessing of Abraham, to thee, and to thy seed with thee; that thou mayest inherit the land wherein thou art a stranger, which God gave unto Abraham (Genesis 28:3-4).

Esau sold his birthright to Jacob and also lost the blessing of his birthright.

Esau came home with his hunted game and cooked a meal for his father, Isaac, only to find out that Jacob had already taken his blessing from Isaac. Esau wept and begged Isaac for any additional blessing for himself. Isaac could not give him the blessing of Abraham or the blessing of the firstborn, but Isaac answered Esau:

And by thy sword shalt thou live, and shalt serve thy brother; and it shall come to pass when thou shalt have the dominion, that thou shalt break his yoke from off thy neck. (Genesis 27:40)

Esau hated Jacob because of the blessing that Isaac blessed Jacob with. Esau sold his birthright to Jacob and also lost the blessing of his birthright. Esau now planned in his heart to kill Jacob (Genesis 27:41).

Jacob became Israel. Even today, Esau hates Israel. Esau does live by the sword, and is a people stronger than Israel. Esau has always been at war with Jacob. The struggle that began in their mother's womb continues. Jacob grabbed hold of Esau's heel when he was born, and ever since, Esau has believed he will crush Jacob under his heel.

Esau Marries into Ishmael

Esau went to Ishmael, his uncle, and married his daughter Mahalath. Ever since then, Esau and Ishmael have been mingled together in covenant.

> Then went Esau unto Ishmael, and took...Mahalath the daughter of Ishmael Abraham's son, the sister of Nebajoth, to be his wife (Genesis 28:9).

Esau had other wives, but that marriage is where Esau and Ishmael began to forge an alliance, which still exists today. Esau went to his uncle, Ishmael, with hatred in his heart for Jacob. Ever since Esau married Ishmael's daughter, the seed of Esau has been mingled with the descendents of Ishmael.

Today, mingled with Ishmael, is Esau, who has always been at war with Jacob (Israel). Ishmael was spoken of as being a man of war, and Esau was destined to live by the sword. They both were archers but with different intentions. Ishmael was an archer for survival in the wilderness war. Esau was a hunter of the wild, more interested in hunting his prey and celebrating his strength over Jacob, the worker of the fields. Esau lived by the sword, and Ishmael was always at war. My intent is not to focus on the literal blood descendents of Esau. Gods loves the descendents of Esau as much as any other people on the

Man divides, but God separates unto Himself.

face of the earth, for God is not a respecter of persons (Romans 2:11). All nations come from one blood and are saved by the blood of Jesus. Man divides, but God separates unto Himself. Noah replenished the earth after the flood, and from seventy nations, God separated unto Himself a people through Abraham, Isaac, and Jacob, who became Israel. So God recognized these two groups (nations) of people as Jews and Gentiles. Later, through the promised seed of Abraham, Isaac, and Jacob, God blessed all the nations of the earth in Christ Jesus, giving birth to the Church: one new man, made of Jew and Gentile alike in faith in Jesus the Messiah. So God loves these three groups of people and is working out His plan for them (1 Corinthians 10:32). However we must gain insight into the spirit or nature of Esau to understand why God is exposing the face of terrorism in Islam today.

> *The cry of Ishmael and the pain of Esau that once united them are now forces that divide them.*

THE SPIRIT OF ESAU: THE CRISIS OF ISLAM

Islam is in a modern-day crisis. What brought Esau and Ishmael together is now bringing a separation in Islam. The cry of Ishmael and the pain of Esau that once united them are now forces that divide them. There are two groups of people among Islam today, those who have the cry of Ishmael in their hearts and those who have the intent of Esau in their hearts. God is exposing the spirit of Esau in the face of terrorism. Terrorism and Islam have become synonymous in the world today. The spirit of Esau is the actual spirit of terrorism in Islam today. The Muslim people can be divided into two groups. In the first group are the majority of Muslims, with the cry of Ishmael in their hearts. They are looking at this terrorism and realizing that Islam has not answered the cry of their own hearts. They are still hungry and thirsty in a spiritual wilderness, looking for God to respond to this crisis in Islam.

The second group are Muslims who have embraced the spirit of Esau and have sold their natural birthright to terrorism, with no regard for life. They are willing to strap a bomb around their chest and die in the hope of waking up in paradise to seventy-two virgins. This spirit is not interested in peace but in terrorism until death. This spirit has been around for generations. This group includes the terrorists and those who favor them. Of course, this group is the minority.

At the heart of this spirit is hatred for Israel, because of the blessing Isaac blessed Jacob with instead of Esau (Genesis 27:41). To gain deeper insight into terrorism, let's recap what the Bible says about Esau. Esau despised his birthright and sold it for a bowl of lentil soup and was tricked out of his blessing as the firstborn of Isaac. He grew up to be a skilled and cunning hunter, who knew how to hunt in the wild, and was a strong man destined to live by the sword (Genesis 27:40). Esau then married into Ishmael, joining with a people who are destined to be at war within and at war with all. Esau became the father of Edom and the Edomites. Islam came through Ishmael's son Kedar, ancestor of the prophet of Islam, to the great nation of Ishmael and to the nation of Esau.

> *The spirit of Esau is the actual spirit of terrorism in Islam today.*

Ishmael's descendents embraced Islam, looking for the answer to the cry of their hearts, and the descendents of Esau embraced Islam as the means of expression of his heart. Today, the spirit of Esau is expressing itself through the face of terrorism in Islam. The heart of Esau or the spirit of Esau is among Ishmael today. This spirit hates Jacob (Israel) and wants to kill him. The cry of the Muslim people goes back 4,000 years to the heart of Ishmael, long before Islam. This cry is still roaring in the hearts of Muslims around the world today. While terrorism is being unveiled in the face of Islam, the Muslim people are finding their cries unanswered.

The Bible: Cure for Terrorism

For we wrestle not against flesh and blood, but against principalities, against powers, against the rulers of the darkness of this world, against spiritual wickedness in high places (Ephesians 6:12).

I learned, a long time ago, that the plans of the Spirit are birthed into this realm through prayer. God's Word is forever settled in Heaven but must be established on Earth. We, as a people, must pray out the plan of God to be established on the earth. We must take authority over the spirit of Esau through prayer. When we pray, God exposes the deceitful strategies of the enemy and makes a way for His purposes to be established. Just as watchmen watch a city, so in the Kingdom, watchmen watch and pray in the Spirit against all principalities and powers and can see what the enemy is trying to do and intercede for those in danger.

The cry of the Muslim people goes back 4,000 years to the heart of Ishmael, long before Islam

Ishmael Shall Be Saved but Esau Judged

There are many Esau hearts who have sold their birthrights in this hour. Jacob came out of his mother's womb holding the heel of Esau. Ever since then, Esau has desired to crush Jacob under his heel, but the God of Jacob (Israel) will crush the spirit of Esau.

"*And saviours shall come up on mount Zion to judge the mount of Esau; and the kingdom shall be the* LORD's" (Obadiah 1:21). The whole book of Obadiah is a vision the prophet had about the present, past and future of Esau and his descendents. Esau and his descendents rejoiced at the destruction and captivity of Israel much like the modern day terrorists celebrate the destruction of their enemies. Notice the word *saviours* in the above verse, speaking of believers in the Jesus the Messiah. According to the book of Hebrews we have come unto mount Zion; the city of the living God, heavenly Jerusalem and unto a kingdom that can not be shaken. These saviours on "mount Zion" are believers who understand the authority of the Kingdom they represent on earth. They recognize the kingdoms of this world shall become the kingdoms of the Most High God. The *mount of Esau* represents the government of Esau, which is the spirit of Esau or spirit of terrorism in Islam today. So believers must pray and intercede from their seated position of authority in Christ, making way for the government of God to crush the spirit of Esau in this hour.

This spirit has camouflaged the destiny of Muslim people, making us deaf to the cry of Ishmael

"*And the God of peace shall bruise Satan under your feet shortly*" (Romans 16:20). The spirit of Esau hopes to camouflage the identity of Ishmael and abort his destiny. Simultaneously, this spirit of terrorism seeks to paralyze the Church with a fear of reaching out to Muslims. This spirit holds many people hostage and is abusing the hidden treasure of Ishmael.

Many focus on Esau while God waits to hear the cry of Ishmael so He may show the Muslim people the face of Jesus Christ.

> *For thus had the Lord said unto me, Within a year, according to the years of an hireling, and all the glory of Kedar shall fail: And the residue of the number of archers, the mighty men of the children of Kedar, shall be diminished: for the LORD God of Israel hath spoken it* (Isaiah 21:16-17).

Kedar was the second son of Ishmael, ancestor to Mohammad, the prophet of Islam. These archers and mighty men seem to carry the description of the modern-day terrorist. The nature of the spirit of Esau is that of a hunter and archer who seeks out his prey and attacks with no value for life. Esau kept his wrath forever against Jacob and the symbol of his wrath was always the sword aimed at Israel.

> *Thus saith the LORD; For three transgressions of Edom, and for four, I will not turn away the punishment thereof; because he did pursue his brother with the sword, and did cast off all pity, and his anger did tear perpetually, and he kept his wrath for ever* (Amos 1:11).

The controversial element of the sword among the Muslim people is courtesy of the spirit of Esau. This spirit has camouflaged the destiny of Muslim people, making us deaf to the cry of Ishmael and blind to the face of Ishmael. God, with one hand, is reaching out to Ishmael and, with the other hand, is judging the spirit of Esau. The spirit of Esau is looking for new followers and a whole generation of Muslims lies in the valley of decision, frustrated with a cry unanswered.

"I am going to visit the Muslim people in dreams and visions and re-awaken the cry of their hearts so that they will seek Me out for the answers."

Chapter Five

Ishmael and the Father

We learned in the earlier chapters that God named Ishmael before he was born because his destiny was hidden in his name (*Ishmael* means *God hears*). Thousands of years ago, Ishmael was left under a bush in the wilderness, but God heard the voice of the lad and opened the eyes of Hagar to a well of water to give him to drink that he might live. We are living in a time when Ishmael is crying out to God. God will hear his cry and open his eyes and show him the well of everlasting life. The Church must pray that God will create a cry in the heart of the Muslim people so deep that it touches the heart of the Most High. We, the Church of God, must intercede for Ishmael like a mother would for a dying child. For God uses the Church to birth the plans of the Spirit into this realm through prayer. Today, when God hears the cry of Ishmael, He will use another lady, the Church, to give him water from the well of everlasting life. It took water to save his life from death in the wilderness, and today, it will take living water to save him from death unto life eternal. Jesus has always been a fisher of men and desires to make us fishers of men so that we will be ready for this season of harvest.

God is going to use the conversion of Ishmael to stir up the Church as God used the conversion of Saul to stir up the early Church in the midst of persecution. God will use Ishmael to provoke the Church unto a passion for Jesus, for what the Church has forsaken, Ishmael will embrace. God is going to use Ishmael to provoke Israel to jealousy for the Messiah. Thus far, we have been talking about what is going to happen, why it is significant to the times we are living in, and whom it will affect. Now I am going to share with you how all this will evolve.

> *The Lamb of God was slain before the foundation of the world, but only manifested on Earth in the fullness of time.*

When God began to open my eyes concerning His plan for the Muslim people in these last days, I was excited to see how this plan would unfold and I am sure you are too.

SEASONS AND TIMES

First, we must recognize that the plan of God works in its season. For example the Lamb of God was slain before the foundation of the world, but only manifested on Earth in the fullness of time or the appointed season. The plan of God is forever settled in Heaven, but there is a season for it to be established on Earth. God moves in appointed seasons of time. It is one thing to know what God is saying; it is another to discern the season He is speaking about. A Kairos moment opens the door to destiny, and that which has been hidden for ages is revealed. When time and eternity come together, the season of fulfillment and the Word of the Lord meet. Once the season is unveiled and the Word is revealed, all that is left to do is to respond. This Kairos moment has already begun over the Muslim world.

DREAMS AND VISIONS

I asked God how He would do all this. He started out by saying "I am going to do it with dreams and visions. I am going to visit the Muslim people in dreams and visions and re-awaken the cry of their hearts so that they will seek Me out for the answers." God will respond to the cry of Ishmael with dreams and visions of Jesus. In search of the truth about these visions, the Muslims are going to come to the Church looking for answers. The answer to these dreams and visions will be the Gospel of Christ, which is the power of God unto salvation. Imagine millions of Muslims looking for answers to their visions about Jesus, the man clothed in white with holes in his hands saying *"I am the way, the truth, and the life"* (John 14:6). These dreams and visions will grip their consciousness, and their hearts will forever long to search out the Father that is drawing them. I know from experience that Muslims pay extra attention to their dreams, because they believe God can speak to them through their dreams. Muslims believe God has not spoken since the death of Mohammad, the prophet of Islam, thus leaving dreams as an avenue of communication to their hearts. Jesus will appear in visions and dreams to the Muslim people across the earth in this precious season. We have been receiving reports consistently that the primary way that Muslims start their journey in receiving Jesus as Lord is through a dream or a vision. It has already begun, and it is going to increase exceedingly. The Holy Spirit will reveal the word of truth to their hearts in dreams and visions. God gave

Pharaoh a dream that left him restless in search of the truth. The dream so gripped his consciousness that he sought out Joseph from prison to understand the truth (Genesis 41:14). There are men like Pharaoh in the business world and in governments of the Islamic world who God is going to reach through dreams and visions of Jesus. They will be key instruments in creating platforms for the Gospel to reach behind closed doors. Joseph was prepared in the Holy Spirit to access the wisdom of God, and we as the Church must be prepared and positioned to move with God. Maybe you have been in prison with an unfulfilled dream, deprived of your destiny, but God is about to bring you out into a wealthy place where your gift will be in demand by the Pharaohs of the world. For that which you have been prepared for all your life is about to manifest before you. God is speaking to people through dreams and visions of Jesus to get their attention.

God gave Pharaoh a dream that left him restless in search of the truth.

We are living in a dispensation of the new covenant where God is putting the law into the minds and hearts of people even through dreams and visions (Jeremiah 31:33). The Holy Spirit, speaking through Peter, reminds us of the Word of the Lord:

> *And it shall come to pass in the last days, saith God, I will pour out of my Spirit upon all flesh: and your sons and your daughters shall prophesy, and your young men shall see visions, and your old men shall dream dreams: And on my servants and on my handmaidens I will pour out in those days of my Spirit; and they shall prophesy (Acts 2:17-18).*

We must be ready to preach the Gospel to them, for the Gospel of Christ is the power of God unto salvation. Simultaneously, God will provoke Ishmael. Nothing provokes the Muslims more to anger than ex-Muslims preaching the Gospel to others right before their eyes. But these same Muslims will seek out answers to their questions from the westerners. God is going to bring Muslim converts to the fore-front in this hour.

TELEVISION AND MEDIA

God has opened the gates that previously kept the Gospel out of the nation of Islam. The wall in the spirit that kept the Gospel out of the nation of Islam has fallen and we must align ourselves with the season we are living in. Just like communism fell, Islam has also fallen. You may not be able to see it yet, but it has already happened and soon it will be common knowledge. The heavens are opening up over the Muslim world, making way for the rain of the Spirit to fall over thirsty Muslim hearts. God is going to use media, television, and satellite immeasurably in this hour to reach the Muslims. While men are yet speaking, the Holy Ghost will fall on those who hear the Word (Acts 10:44). The Muslims are hungry for the bread of Heaven. The cloud of glory will invade their homes and reveal Jesus to them through satellite and media. Some will have dreams and visions of Jesus, and others will be awestruck by the glory of God, while sitting in front of television. We are able ministers of the New Testament, not of the letter that kills but of the

> *The wall in the spirit that kept the Gospel out of the nation of Islam has fallen.*

spirit that gives life. We are dispensers of the life of God, not of mere knowledge but the very likeness of God that is a light unto men. One of the characteristics of the new covenant in Jeremiah was that God would write the laws on the hearts of men and put His laws into the very minds of men. So while ministers of the new covenant are yet speaking by the Holy Spirit, the very hearts of those who hear the Word will be engraved with truth from Heaven. Indeed, we have a better covenant established on better promises. Jesus will do great miracles in the homes of Muslims (and others) through television and media. Church, get ready: a whole generation of Muslims are coming into the Kingdom of God.

Light takes care of darkness, but the glory takes care of gross darkness.

THE GLORY OF GOD

Arise, shine; for thy light is come, and the glory of the LORD is risen upon thee. For, behold, the darkness shall cover the earth, and gross darkness the people: but the LORD shall arise upon thee, and his glory shall be seen upon thee (Isaiah 60:1-2).

Light takes care of darkness, but the glory takes care of gross darkness. In Matthew chapter six, Jesus says that if the light in us is darkness, how great is that darkness. Luke 11:35 tells us to take heed that the light in us be not darkness. People who have never heard the Gospel are in darkness. When people hear the Gospel yet believe in another god, that is gross darkness. The light in them has become great darkness. Every religion has light (knowledge), but we have life that is light unto men. *"In him was life; and the life was the light of men"* (John 1:4). Life is the revelation of Jesus to the heart, and light is the illumination or understanding of that revelation to the mind. The gross darkness in Isaiah 60:2 and the great darkness in Matthew chapter six are one and the same, except one is upon and the other is within. The revelation of Jesus to the heart and the illumination of Jesus to the mind will remove great darkness from within. When the earth sees the glory cover the Church, then the gross darkness that covers the people will be removed. Light is for darkness and the glory is for gross darkness.

We must be living epistles read of all men. We must, with open faces, behold in the mirror the revelation of the glory of the Lord and be changed into the same image of Jesus, from one degree of glory to another, by the Spirit of God (2 Corinthians 3:18). When they see us, they must see Jesus. *"Look unto me, and be ye saved, all the ends of the earth: for I am God and there is none else"* (Isaiah 45:22). Jesus is the head and we are the body. How else can the earth see God except by seeing His glory upon the Church? When those on Earth see His glory, they will see Jesus. When they see Jesus, they will know the Father. *"Every knee should bow...and...every tongue should confess that Jesus Christ is Lord"* (Philippians 2:10-11).

> *When the earth sees the glory cover the church, then the gross darkness that covers the people will be removed*

The Son has been heard, but the time has come for the Son to be seen. The will of the Father is that all who see and hear the Son believe (John 6:40). The glory of God shall rise upon us, and we shall speak as the oracles of God. By the Spirit of God through plainness of speech, we will reveal the wisdom of God in the face of Jesus to the world. That wisdom was hidden in a mystery until the beginning of the Church age. Now, at the end of the age, that wisdom will be made manifest to all men by the Church. The Spirit of God revealed it then to the Church. Now He shall reveal it to the world through the Church, with the intent that even principalities and powers in heavenly places might know the manifold wisdom of God (Ephesians 3:10). We must know every dimension of the love of Christ, beyond mere knowledge, so that we may be filled with all the fullness of God (Ephesians 3:19).

> *The abundance of the sea shall be converted unto thee, the forces of the Gentiles shall come unto thee* (Isaiah 60:5).

God named Ishmael before he was born, with the end in mind, knowing one day there would be 1.6 billion Muslims in the world awaiting the call to their destiny. They represent nearly 42 percent of the world's unsaved population.

MIRACLES, SIGNS, AND WONDERS

Knowing that one day there would be 1.6 billion Muslims in the world awaiting the call to their destiny.

There is a realm of the supernatural above the earthly politics and red tape of ministry. This is the realm of miracles, signs, and wonders. It involves more than just knowing the acts of God but also the ways of God. The children of Israel knew the acts of God yet died in the wilderness, but Moses knew the ways of God and saw His Gory. It is about living in the realm of heaven and visiting Earth rather than living on Earth and visiting Heaven. It is not a realm of visitation but a realm of habitation. It is a realm where you see Earth through the eyes of Heaven. It is a realm of faith where you see the invisible and do the impossible. It is a realm where you no longer follow the acts of God but where the acts of God follow you. It is a state of being where you are not just *under* the cloud of God but *in* the cloud of God. It not just about *seeing* the pillar of fire by night but it is about *being* the pillar of fire by night in Christ Jesus. His ministers ought to be flames of fire. It is not just about the miracles, but it is about the Spirit in which you live, move, and have your being. It is more about where you walk than what you see. Man has always asked God to come down to where he is, but God is asking us to come up to where **He is.** God comes to the place where we are, but there is a higher place in the Spirit where He is. This is the realm we are born of and destined to live and walk in. In this realm we breathe the presence of God and manifest the life of God. In this realm we are not impressed by miracles but are rather in awe of the majesty of God. It is not just the outer court, where we hear the Word, or the inner court, where we walk in the Word, but the Holy of Holies, where we become the Word. It is where we become living epistles read of all men. It is a realm where we don't just preach the message but become the message.

It is a realm of faith where you see the invisible and do the impossible

We are living in an hour when God is raising up a generation that will speak as the oracle of God while in the cloud of glory. While men are yet speaking, the Holy Ghost will fall on those who hear the Word. It is not a realm of enticing words of man's wisdom but a realm of demonstration and power of the Holy Ghost. While Philip was yet preaching, demons left people. It is a realm in which demons tremble and strongholds are broken. It is a realm where devils tremble and flee rather than fight. It is a realm of the glory of God. It is a realm where we are *not* and *Jesus is*. It is a secret place where your identity is hidden in Christ alone. It is a realm where man can no longer be seen because all that is seen is the glory of God. It is a realm where man cannot deny the existence and majesty of God. The whole earth shall be covered with the glory of God as the waters cover the sea. The density of God's presence will be immeasurable and the lightning of God will flash through the souls of men.

> *It is a realm where we are* not *and Jesus* is.

Miracles, signs and wonders are more a result of living and walking in the Spirit with God.

RAISING THE DEAD

The Holy Spirit will move with innumerable miracles, demonstrations of power, and wonders to draw the attention of man to Jesus Christ. We will see a massive operation and manifestation of the gifts of the Spirit in this hour. The power gifts especially will be in operation for the purpose of winning souls into the Kingdom. God will show forth His glory through mighty signs, wonders, and acts of the Holy Ghost, including many dead being raised to life, but there will also be swift judgment and some will even drop dead like Ananias and Sapphira (Acts 5:5-9).

Muslims believe that Jesus never really died and therefore was never raised from the dead. Muslims believe that no one can raise the dead except Jesus. Muslims believe God Almighty gave this power only to Jesus while He was on the earth. As far as they are concerned, Jesus is in Heaven, not on Earth, and so no one can perform such miracles. So when we raise the dead in Jesus' name by the power of God, Muslims immediately realize that Jesus is real and the Bible is true. When they see the dead raised, it confirms the resurrection power of Jesus Christ. Muslims believe Allah can do all other miracles, but the raising of the dead was reserved for Jesus. Such miracles give witness to the life and resurrection of Jesus Christ.

We will see a massive operation and manifestation of the gifts of the Spirit in this hour

WITCHCRAFT

Many people from third-world countries see witch doctors and warlocks and other spiritualists perform lying signs and wonders. To people in those places, an unconfirmed Gospel is not good enough. God's power demonstrated over witchcraft and demonic powers is another key area to the Muslims. They have no way to cast out devils and, in such times of desperation, will seek help from outside their faith; whereas Hindus worship devils and will sacrifice to idols if they have to rid themselves of such trouble. Muslims refer to demons as *Gin* and have no power against them. The only thing they can do is find someone who is a medium that deals with stronger demons and hope to find relief. Muslims are really afraid of evil powers and curses. They recognize they have no power against such onslaughts. Therefore, power demonstrated in the name of Jesus Christ over such circumstances is a great witness to the Gospel.

Let me share a story from my last trip to Pakistan. The minute I arrived in Pakistan, there was an unusual grace upon me. I encountered a witch doctor trying to do witchcraft on me. The hand of Lord came upon me for three hours, and I was under the weightiness of God's glory. After that, I got up and went to the witch doctor's house, and as she opened the door, her face turned extremely pale and she began to shake and backed up and was afraid. The power of God was upon me and I did not even do anything. She watched as all the evil spirits began to leave the room. I perceived the same. She was shocked and made me promise to come back for another meeting before I left for Canada. In the meantime, she went to see other more powerful witch doctors to continue her attack against me. The power of God came upon me again and I was in the glory of God. After a few hours, I got up and called her son to pick me up so I could go meet with her as I promised. The son came and picked me up to drive me to her house again. A few minutes before we reached the house, he stopped the car. He confessed to me that when he told the witch doctor I was coming, she begged him not to bring me and ran out of the house, scared. She realized that the power of Jesus was far greater than any demonic evil. Praise God, greater is **He** who is in us than he who is in the world (1 John 4:4). Amen.

As a Muslim, I believed that Abraham took Ishmael to the altar of sacrifice instead of Isaac.

Chapter Six

Ishmael and Isaac

God blessed Ishmael but established his covenant with Isaac. Isaac was the child of promise with whom God instituted His covenant for an everlasting covenant and this included his seed after him.

As a Muslim, I believed that Abraham took Ishmael to the altar of sacrifice instead of Isaac. This is the cornerstone of the Muslim beliefs. The Dome of the Rock sits on the very mount where Abraham took his son. In this chapter, I desire to present the truth as it is shown in the Bible concerning Ishmael and Isaac. Every Muslim should have a chance to know what the Bible says about Ishmael and Isaac. Let us study the Biblical account:

> And it came to pass after these things, that God did tempt Abraham, and said unto him, Abraham: and he said, Behold, here I am. And he said, **Take now thy son, thine only son Isaac,** whom thou lovest, and get thee into the land of Moriah; and offer him there for a burnt offering upon one of

the mountains which I will tell thee of. And Abraham rose up early in the morning, and saddled his ass, and took two of his young men with him, and Isaac his son, and clave the wood for the burnt offering, and rose up, and went unto the place of which God had told him (Genesis 22:1-3 emphasis added).

The first thing we must take notice is that Abraham had already cast out Ishmael with Hagar and left him with no inheritance in the wilderness. Ishmael was cast out right after Isaac was weaned. Isaac was no more than three years old. It was several years after Ishmael was cast out when God decided to test Abraham. Ishmael was not even there! Second, I would like you to notice that God deliberately referred to Isaac as Abraham's only son. After Abraham came closer to the mount, he and Isaac went up alone to worship the Lord.

Notice that God deliberately referred to Isaac as Abraham's only son.

Then on the third day Abraham lifted up his eyes, and saw the place afar off. And Abraham said unto his young men, Abide ye here with the ass; and I and the lad will go yonder and worship, and come again to you (Genesis 22:4-5 emphasis added).

Notice Abraham told the young men he would go with the lad and come back again. He was planning on coming back with Isaac. Abraham believed God would raise Isaac from the dead to fulfill His promise (*"In Isaac shall thy seed be called"*) to him.

*By faith Abraham, when he was tried, offered up Isaac: and he that had received the promises offered up his **only begotten son**, Of whom it was said, That in Isaac shall thy seed be called: Accounting that God was able to raise him up, even from the dead; from whence also he received him in a figure* (Hebrews 11:17-19, emphasis added).

Once again, the Holy Spirit, in the book of Hebrews, refers to Isaac as Abraham's one and only son. Let the truth be established in the mouths of two witnesses. Abraham, by faith, in a figurative sense received Isaac back from the dead. As far as Abraham was concerned, his son was sacrificed unto God and potentially dead. He was serious and took a three-day journey with fire and wood and a knife ready to carry out the sacrifice as an act of obedience.

And Abraham took the wood of the burnt offering, and laid it upon Isaac his son; and he took the fire in his hand, and a knife; and they went both of them together. And Isaac spake unto Abraham his father, and said, My father: and he said, Here am I, my son. And he said, Behold the fire and the wood: but where is the lamb for a burnt offering? And Abraham said, My son, God will provide himself a lamb for a burnt offering: so they went both of them together (Genesis 22:6-8).

When he answered his son Isaac, Abraham as a prophet of God saw into the future and declared that God would Himself provide a lamb. He prophetically spoke of the Lamb of God that would come to take away the sins of the world.

And they came to the place which God had told him of; and Abraham built an altar there, and laid

91

the wood in order, and bound Isaac his son, and laid him on the altar upon the wood. And Abraham stretched forth his hand, and took the knife to slay his son. And the angel of the LORD called unto him out of heaven, and said, Abraham, Abraham: and he said, Here am I. And he said, Lay not thine hand upon the lad, neither do thou any thing unto him: for now I know that thou fearest God, seeing thou hast not withheld thy son, thine only son from me. And Abraham lifted up his eyes, and looked, and behold behind him a ram caught in a thicket by his horns: and Abraham went and took the ram, and offered him up for a burnt offering in the stead of his son (Genesis 22:9-13).

Just before Abraham was about to slay his son, the angel of the Lord called out to him and stopped him. God had provided a ram for Abraham to offer in place of his only son Isaac.

*And the angel of the LORD called unto Abraham out of heaven the second time, And said, By myself have I sworn, saith the LORD, **for because thou hast done this thing, and hast not withheld thy son, thine only son:** That in blessing I will bless thee, and in multiplying I will multiply thy seed as the stars of the heaven, and as the sand which is upon the sea shore; and thy seed shall possess the gate of his enemies; And in thy seed shall all the nations of the earth be blessed; because thou hast obeyed my voice* (Genesis 22:15-18 emphasis added).

Abraham did not withhold his only son Isaac on the mount of sacrifice. For this reason God swore by Himself an oath that, in Isaac, all the nations of the earth would be blessed. Abraham already had the promise, but now he had an oath as an irrefutable guarantee. Ishmael was blessed, but the covenant was made with Isaac, the child of promise, and with his seed after him.

THE SEED

God keeps referring to a seed, not all the seeds of Abraham, but to a single seed. This seed that God keeps referring to throughout the Bible was first spoken of in the days of Adam. After the fall of Adam, God prophesied that a seed of the woman would come forth and bruise the head of the Satan with his heel. Jesus is the seed of the woman and He is the seed of Abraham, Isaac, and Jacob. He is the seed of David and He is the promised seed through which the whole earth is blessed.

God keeps refer-ring to a seed: not all the seeds of Abraham, but a single seed.

A CHILD IS BORN BUT A SON GIVEN

For unto us a child is born, unto us a son is given: and the government shall be upon his shoulder: and his name shall be called Wonderful, Counsellor, The mighty God, The everlasting Father, The Prince of Peace (Isaiah 9:6).

Muslims do not understand how Jesus could be the Son of God. They assume Christians believe that Jesus became the Son of God after being born of the virgin Mary. The above Scripture is speaking of Jesus. It says that unto us a child is born but a Son is given. Jesus was born a child, but He was the Son of God before He ever came to Earth and was born of a woman. God

93

gave His only begotten Son. The Son of God was given not born. Jesus is before all things and existed with the Father and was in the Father before all creation. Let us continue to get some insight from the Word of God concerning Jesus:

> *Who is the image of the invisible God, the firstborn of every creature: For by him were all things created, that are in heaven, and that are in earth, visible and invisible, whether they be thrones, or dominions, or principalities, or powers: all things were created by him, and for him: And he is before all things, and by him all things consist* (Colossians 1:15-17).

All things were created by Him and for Him and through Him alone they exist. Jesus is the **Word Of God**. He is the living Word of God.

> *In the beginning was the Word, and the Word was with God, and the Word was God* (John 1:1).

To better grasp the meaning of this verse, I am going to dissect it into three parts.

In the beginning was the Word

The first part of the verse goes back into eternity when God created all things that we see and don't see. We know that all things were created by the Word

The Word was with God

The second part of verse goes even further back before anything was ever created, and even then the Word was with God.

The Word was God

The third part of the verse goes even further back when the Word was in God. This is before the Word came out of God.

94

The same was in the beginning with God. All things were made by him; and without him was not any thing made that was made (John 1:2-3, emphasis added).

In the first part of the third verse, the Word is referred to as "Him." Now we begin to see that the Word is a person. This person is Jesus Christ, the Son of God. He is the Word that came out of God, the Word that was with God and the Word by whom all things were created both seen and unseen. He is the image of the invisible God. He is the express image of the Father and the brightness of the glory of God. We are talking about Jesus before He even came to the earth. This person, the Word, came into the world that was made by Him and unto a people that He gave light (life) to, but those people did not know Him.

> *He is the Word that came out of God, by whom all things were created both seen and unseen.*

That was the true Light, which lighteth every man that cometh into the world. He was in the world, and the world was made by him, and the world knew him not (John 1:9-10).

This Word then became flesh and took the embodiment of flesh to literally walk among us. This Word was born of a virgin and came as a man and lived among us.

And the Word was made flesh, and dwelt among us, (and we beheld his glory, the glory as of the only begotten of the Father,) full of grace and truth (John 1:14).

This Word then revealed unto us the glory of the invisible God. This Word is a person and His name is Jesus Christ.

> *And of his fulness have all we received, and grace for grace. For the law was given by Moses, but grace and truth came by Jesus Christ. No man hath seen God at any time, the only begotten Son, which is in the bosom of the Father, he hath declared him* (John 1:16-18).

Jesus is the revelation of the Father, who loves us and sent His Son, Jesus Christ, as the Lamb of God to die for our sins while He Himself was sinless. This same Jesus was crucified, dead, and buried until the third day. Early in the morning of the third day, the Father who sent Him raised Him from the dead to live forever. This risen Jesus is at the right hand of God in Heaven making intercession for us. Jesus is real, and if you were to call on His name, you too would find salvation in Him. He is the living Word and our Savior and Lord.

God is going to give creative ideas to the Body of Christ that will position believers in places of financial domin-ion in times of famine in the world.

Chapter Seven

The Blessing of Ishmael

I believe that the Holy Spirit is speaking to leaders in the Body of Christ concerning wealth and finances for Kingdom purposes. Many have a keen sense that a great transfer of wealth is coming to the Church to transact Kingdom business. I believe God is giving men and women unconventional ideas about ministry and finances in the 21st century. God is raising up apostles and prophets in these last days who will have their own oil wells to deliver the Word of the Lord. They will have the financial resources to establish God's covenant on the earth. God is going to give creative ideas to the Body of Christ that will position believers in places of financial dominion in times of famine in the world. There will be a dominion anointing to function in the marketplace that will marvel skeptics in the business world. God is about to bring many into a wealthy place so they can be positioned to fund the greatest harvest man has ever seen.

God is not going to place the command of such wealth into the hands of people who do not know their purpose in the Kingdom. It is necessary to know the purpose for which you were created and to recognize the gift that is within you to fulfill your destiny. Revelation of purpose precedes the manifestation of provision. Once we know the purpose for which we were destined, an uncompromising passion is born. Divine purpose gives birth to authentic passion which, in turn, stirs up the gift of God within us. When the gift within us is stirred, it always brings prosperity to accomplish the God-given purpose in our lives, leaving more than enough to help finance other God-given ideas in the Kingdom. God sent us into the world not to accumulate money but for this purpose, that we glorify God and serve one another in love. Money is merely a tool that can be used for a good purpose or a bad one; it just takes on the nature of the man it is entrusted to.

Revelation of purpose precedes the manifestation of provision.

We must understand our purpose with a Kingdom mentality. A Kingdom mentality realizes that our God-given purpose is to enhance the Kingdom of God and not our own kingdom or agenda. A Kingdom mentality is about stewardship rather than ownership. We are merely stewards of the resources entrusted to us to establish His covenant. In the Kingdom, we own nothing yet partake of everything that God has in Christ.

> *But thou shalt remember the LORD thy God: for it is he that giveth thee power to get wealth, that he may establish his covenant which he sware unto thy fathers, as it is this day* (Deuteronomy 8:18).

God gives us the power to get wealth, but we must not forget that it is for the purpose of establishing His covenant on the earth. This is the same covenant that God made with Abraham to bless all the families of the earth through his seed whom we know as the Lord Jesus Christ. How do we in our lives specifically establish the covenant? We do that by fulfilling the destiny for which we were created and placed on this earth. We can only establish His covenant on the earth by specifically doing that which we were destined to do. The purpose of God is in us, and every purpose of God is redemptive in nature and will directly or indirectly advance the Gospel. Some may be called to the five-fold ministry, while others are called to establish television stations and satellites as a medium to proclaim the Gospel. Someone designs, another engineers, and yet another manufactures technology for our use every day. Of course, television is not dedicated to the use of God, but in a fallen world, neither are computers, radio, internet, airplanes, automobiles, and so on. The list is just endless. Let us not be limited in our thinking. We are living in the world, but we are not of the world. Let us be established in our understanding that the power to get wealth goes hand-in-hand with the purpose for which we are destined on this earth. Why give up everything to the devil and let him use it, when it is meant to be used for the Kingdom of God?

> *We can only establish His covenant on the earth by specifically doing that which we were destined to do..*

GOD'S PURPOSE IN BLESSING ISHMAEL

We know God's works are clothed with purpose. God's provision is always hidden in His blessing. I would like to share with you about the role of Ishmael in the end-time wealth transfer:

And as for Ishmael, I have heard thee: Behold, I have blessed him, and will make him fruitful, and will multiply him exceedingly; twelve princes shall he beget, and I will make him a great nation (Genesis 17:20).

Ishmael was deprived of the blessing of Abraham and any inheritance when he was cast out in the wilderness with Hagar. God did bless Ishmael with an unconditional blessing; as a result, this blessing has accumulated and wealth has been stored up in the Muslim world. Just in the Middle East alone, more than twice the world's total known oil reserves exist. They supply more than double the oil of the rest of the world combined.

For years, Ishmael's oil wells have been storing up wealth in the Muslim world that has spilled into the commerce and the business communities worldwide. They are very careful to support other Muslim businesses first, much like the Jewish communities. Muslims are forbidden in the Qur'an to charge interest, and Muslim lending organizations do not charge interest to other Muslims on mortgages and loans. That way, their homes get paid off quicker and they have more equity in their homes and are able to invest in more property. They also believe in owning land, property, and real estate everywhere they go. The Muslim people have been zealous about both their religious and their

> *The Muslim people have been zealous about both their religious and their economic dominions.*

economic dominions. There is an enormous amount of wealth that has been stored up for thousands of years in the Muslim world and is still being stored up today. From the earliest days on, the Ishmaelites were businessmen who traded in the marketplace with caravans of goods. Commerce was a way of life for them. This wealth has been stored up for a purpose.

He has provision for His purpose hidden in His blessing.

God blessed Ishmael thousands of years ago, knowing that when he would come into the Kingdom, the treasure hidden in dark places and the secret treasure that is stored up will come into the Kingdom, to finance the Gospel in part. Even the oil in the wells will be for the Gospel's sake. *He has provision for His purpose hidden in His blessing.* God blessed Ishmael unconditionally with the intention to fund the end-time harvest in part. We will see enormous wealth transfer from the Muslim world in the billions and trillions. God preserved the oil and raw materials in the earth for resources to establish His covenant. He created the earth in its fullness and all that is in the earth belongs to Him. God gives the power to get wealth for the sole purpose to establish His covenant, and God blessed Ishmael for the establishment of His covenant in the end times.

THE GLORY AND THE GOLD

The Church has always wondered about the oil in the Middle East and the financial backing of Islam. In the meantime, we have taken for granted the oil of the Spirit that we possess. Ishmael longs to be refreshed with fresh oil from Heaven. There is going to be an exchange of oil in these last days. The oil in the Middle East will be exchanged for the oil in the Kingdom of God. God desires to bring the streams of oil together. Wealth and substance coming into the Kingdom is not foreign. Let us gain insight into the Word of God:

> Arise, shine; for thy light is come, and the glory of the LORD is risen upon thee. For, behold, the darkness shall cover the earth, and gross darkness the people: but the LORD shall arise upon thee, and his glory shall be seen upon thee. And the Gentiles shall come to thy light, and kings to the brightness of thy rising (Isaiah 60:1-3).

As we study the above Scriptures, we see the glory of God coming upon the Church and the manifestation of this glory causing nations and kings to come into the Kingdom.

> Then thou shalt see, and flow together, and thine heart shall fear, and be enlarged; because the abundance of the sea shall be converted unto thee, the forces of the Gentiles shall come unto thee. The multitude of camels shall cover thee, the dromedaries of Midian and Ephah; all they from Sheba shall come: they shall bring gold and incense; and they shall shew forth the praises of the LORD. All the flocks of Kedar shall be gathered together unto thee, the rams of Nebaioth shall minister unto thee: they shall come up with acceptance on mine altar, and I will glorify the house of my glory (Isaiah 60:5-7).

In verse five, we see that the wealth and treasure of the Gentiles will come into the Kingdom. Muslims represent 42 percent of the Gentiles today. In verses six and seven, we see a description of the forces of the Gentiles that will come into our hands. Kedar was the second son of Ishmael and ancestor to Mohammad, the prophet of Islam. The Scripture says that all the flocks of Kedar, speaking of the people and the wealth and substance of Ishmael, will transfer into the Kingdom. Muslims have always directed their wealth toward their religious beliefs and the expansion of Islam through the building of mosques and so on. Once their eyes are opened, they will catch the vision of God's heart and continue to passionately support the Gospel. When Ishmael is revived in the presence of God, he will lay his treasures at the feet of Jesus and embrace his destiny.

When Ishmael is revived in the presence of God, he will lay his treasures at the feet of Jesus and embrace his destiny.

FROM TERRORISM

Among the Muslim people, as we have discussed, are those who have embraced the spirit of Esau in the face of terrorism, and they are funding terrorism with their accumulated wealth. Billions go into terrorism, weapons, and training and to the families of suicide bombers in recognition of their deeds. The spirit of Esau has abused part of the wealth of Ishmael. As God judges the spirit of Esau and answers the cry of Ishmael, the flow of money will be directed into the Gospel. As light comes forth concerning the destiny of Ishmael and the purpose of his blessing, then the wealth transfer will occur in its fullness. Revelation of purpose always exceeds the manifestation of provision.

Muslim wealth has been transferred from generation to generation, and in this last generation, there will be a movement of God that will bring that inherited wealth into the Kingdom.

MARKETPLACE TRANSACTIONS

God will cause men in business to rise up, and He will give them wisdom and witty inventions to transact billions with the Muslim countries. There are men whom God is raising up who will have cutting-edge market ideas for the Muslim world. This movement of God will touch Muslim billionaires and open their eyes to the divine purpose behind their blessing. God will connect these people with Kingdom businessmen and billions will be transacted. To the everyday world, it will be business as usual, but in reality, it will be a strategic business plan for the Kingdom of God.

> *This movement of God will touch Muslim billionaires and open their eyes to the divine purpose behind their blessing.*

HIDDEN TREASURES

And I will give thee the treasures of darkness, and hidden riches of secret places, that thou mayest know that I, the LORD, which call thee by thy name, am the God of Israel (Isaiah 45:3).

There is more than enough hidden wealth in the world to finance the Gospel all over the world a million times over. It is just a matter of who possesses it. Wealth can either change hands or the people who hold it can change. Either way, it will be used to establish the covenant of God. Our God, in His wisdom, has always intended to pay for His purposes through the blessing He empowers man with. The blessing is a spiritual endowment but blessings are a natural result of that spiritual empowerment of a person. God blessed Abraham to be a blessing to the whole world in Christ Jesus. Likewise, God blessed Ishmael, knowing that one day he would finance the Gospel in part. That wealth has been stored up for generations and now will be released into the Kingdom. Provision favors the blessed.

What we are destined to do will not be accomplished apart from divine relationships in the Kingdom.

UNITY

Divine purposes are always bigger than one man. No purpose of God is meant to be accomplished alone. Even Jesus did not fulfill the will of God alone. What we are destined to do will not be accomplished apart from divine relationships in the Kingdom. The Body of Christ is made up of believers, and every member of the Body has an important function. When we come together, our comprehension of the purposes of God is synergized and our understanding is fruitful. Unity creates a platform for a commanded blessing (Psalm 133). Unity merges individual destiny with corporate destiny. Corporate destiny brings greater revelation concerning the purposes of God and puts a greater demand on the anointing to get wealth in order to establish His covenant. A body has many parts and each part has its unique function. Every part is needed in order for the body to function in its fullness. Well, the Body of Christ is the same, and we must work together. New wine is always found in a cluster of grapes, and that is where the blessing is (Isaiah 65:8). A grape apart from the cluster is not much good for wine and neither is a believer apart from the Body. Unity is the breeding ground for unlimited potential beyond what we can ask or think, according to the power that works in us (Ephesians 3:20). Unity creates within us the capacity to withstand and utilize greater measures of wealth transfer in order to establish the covenant of God.

Let us ensure that our hearts are united in purpose for the greatest wealth transfer man has ever seen. I believe God blessed Ishmael, not in vain, but for the Gospel's sake in this hour.

God blessed all the nations of the earth in Christ Jesus, giving birth to the Church...

Chapter Eight

The Return of the Lord

All nations come from one blood and are saved by the blood of one, Jesus Christ. Man divides, but God separates unto Himself. Noah replenished the earth after the flood, and from seventy nations, God separated unto Himself a people through Abraham, Isaac, and Jacob, who became Israel. God, throughout the Old Testament, recognized two groups of people, Jews and Gentiles. God blessed all the nations of the earth in Christ Jesus, giving birth to the Church: one new man made of Jew and Gentile alike in faith in Jesus, the Messiah. So God loves these three groups of people and is working out His plan for them (1 Corinthians 10:32).

THE HARVEST

The harvest is ready for reaping. Men and women have gone out to the nations and given up their lives for the cause of the Gospel. Many who have been martyred for Jesus we may never hear about this side of Heaven. Their blood is not forgotten, nor is their labor of love in vain, including missionaries today who have spent all their lives ministering to Muslims and have not seen the fruit they would like to see. It is as if they have toiled all night and have not caught any fish. I believe as you read the following Scriptures you will be encouraged in the Lord. Let me share with you a prophetic picture of the times we are now living in, concerning the harvest:

After these things Jesus shewed himself again to the disciples at the sea of Tiberias; and on this wise shewed he himself. There were together Simon Peter, and Thomas called Didymus, and Nathanael of Cana in Galilee, and the sons of Zebedee, and two other of his disciples. Simon Peter saith unto them, I go a fishing. They say unto him, We also go with thee. They went forth, and entered into a ship immediately; and that night they caught nothing. But when the morning was now come, Jesus stood on the shore: but the disciples knew not that it was Jesus. Then Jesus saith unto them, Children, have ye any meat? They answered him, No. And he said unto them, Cast the net on the right side of the ship, and ye shall find. They cast therefore, and now they were not able to draw it for the multitude of fishes...And the other disciples came in a little ship; (for they were not far from land, but as it were two hundred cubits,) dragging the net with fishes. As soon then as they were come to land, they saw a fire of coals there, and fish laid thereon, and bread. Jesus saith unto them, Bring of the fish which ye have now caught. Simon Peter went up, and drew the net to land full of great fishes, an hundred and fifty and three: and for all there were so many, yet was not the net broken. Jesus saith unto them, Come and dine (John 21:1-12).

Jesus has always desired for us to be fishers of men. He told his disciples he would make them fishers of men. Just like the disciples of Jesus, the Church has been out fishing for generations in the sea of humanity. We even have "ships," speaking of the tools and equipment with which we preach the Gospel, while fishing in the sea of humanity. Yet many have fished through the night and feel like they have not caught any fish. Maybe you have worked all night in the Muslim mission field and have not seen the results you have desired. It is the early morning hour, and Jesus is standing at the shore and maybe you have been unable to recognize Him. But He is telling you to cast your nets on the right side of the ship. We have entered the dawn of a supernatural harvest. We are alive in the dawning of a Kairos moment and experiencing the beginning of a different season. Jesus is asking the Church to cast her nets on the right side of the ship, for He is about to fill her nets with the harvest of multitudes. There will be a supernatural harvest of Muslims and the nations of the world into the Kingdom. We have been fishing with poles, but Jesus is telling us to cast our nets on the right side of the ship. It is time to move from poles to nets. It is time to move from our vision to His vision for the Kingdom. Our vision must expand to encompass the greater purpose of God being worked out in the earth. Corporate vision always enhances personal vision and allows for maximum impact in the Kingdom. Let us look beyond our fishing poles into the face of Jesus and obey His command to cast the net.

> *Just like the disciples of Jesus, the Church has been out fishing for generations in the sea of humanity.*

117

The nets are television, media, satellite, internet, radio, and unconventional ideas. I believe Jesus is giving unconventional instructions to ministries coming forth in this hour. Jesus has been speaking to ministries and churches to unite and form unconventional nets for the harvest. For two thousand years, Jesus has taught men how to be fishers of men, but now He is standing at the shore, causing the fish to flow into our nets, making us fishers of multitudes. We must move from a fisherman mentality to a multitude mentality. Some of you will have to put away your fishing poles and get a hold of the nets in this hour.

God will use these nets in this season to harvest the Muslim people in particular. The wall of Islam has fallen, and the gates are now open for the Gospel to go forth. The time has come for them to come into the Kingdom. We are about to witness a miraculous harvest of souls. Jesus is standing at the shore, calling out to the Church with a command to cast the nets on the right side of the ship. We must obey His command. The disciples obeyed Him and cast the net on the right side of the ship and could not draw the net in because of the quantity of fish. Likewise, we are about to see a supernatural harvest of the multitudes such that we will not be able to contain them in our churches today. This harvest will be so great that we will have to call upon all our brethren to help draw the nets and carry the harvest to shore. Jesus waits at the shore for us and desires for us to bring the fish to Him.

Jesus is the captain of the ship, and we must obey His command

The invitation is open for us all to come to Him. Before we rush to dine with Him, let us obey the command and cast the net and gather the harvest and bring it to Jesus. Then we can dine as much as we want to. How could we leave such a multitude of fish in the sea with Jesus at the shore? There is a fresh anointing being released upon men and women in the Church for a supernatural harvest. Cast the net on the right side of the ship, for a multitude waits your decision. Be not afraid; the net will not break and an overflow of the harvest will come in. The Scripture specifically records that they caught 153 large fish. I believe this specific number can even speak to us beyond

There is a pre-eminent grace of divine perfection being made manifest for this supernatural harvest of the multitudes.

a mere quantity of fish. One is the number of preeminence in the Bible, five is the number of grace, and three is the number of divine perfection. There is a preeminent grace of divine perfection being made manifest for this supernatural harvest of the multitudes. Jesus is standing at the shore; you may not be able to see Him, but can you hear Him?

THE COMING OF THE LORD DRAWETH NIGH

Be patient therefore, brethren, unto the coming of the Lord. Behold, the husbandman waiteth for the precious fruit of the earth, and hath long patience for it, until he receive the early and latter rain. Be ye also patient; stablish your hearts: for the coming of the Lord draweth nigh (James 5:7-8).

Israel awaits the coming of the Messiah, Muslims await the return of Jesus, and the Church is anticipating the soon-coming King. The world is watching the end-time events, and there is great anticipation for the closing of the age. The return of the Lord Jesus is drawing nigh, but God is waiting for the precious fruit of the earth. His eyes are on the harvest, while our eyes are on the clock. A new season is making way for the rains of Heaven to fall upon the harvest fields of the earth. *"The Lord is...not willing that any should perish, but that all should come to repentance"* (2 Peter 3:9). He is calling us, His Church, to divinely cooperate with His grace that is flowing for the nations today, in particular the Islamic nations. Will we cooperate?

Concluding Thoughts

The primary intent of this book is to define and clarify the season we are in, and to bring understanding and create awareness of the significance of Ishmael and his role in provoking Israel to salvation.

However, the full intent of this book is to testify of God's mercy and provision so that none will perish but that all will come to repentance. In many ways, this book serves to provoke us to think outside of our boxes and embrace God's plan for salvation of the nations of the earth. It is a testimony to the truth that the earth will be filled with the knowledge of the glory of our God.

Will we be like the sons of Issachar and discern this season (1 Chronicles 12:32)? If we do, our walk will be graced with wisdom and empowered by revelation, partnering with Heaven, to see the greatest harvest yet seen.

Let us embrace the prophetic truth revealed in this book as a forerunner of something mightier that is yet to come!

Prayer to Know God

I n reading this book, the desire in your heart to know God as Father may have stirred deeply within you. Maybe you would like to genuinely experience His love, forgiveness and acceptance. God desires to open your eyes and show you the specific purpose for which you were designed. Destiny within you is longing to be unlocked by truth in the person of Jesus. If you would like to begin a relationship with God, then say this prayer out loud in your own words:

Dear Heavenly Father, you are the Most High God, and I come to you in the name of Jesus. I thank you for sending Jesus to the earth as the Word of God who became flesh. Father, I receive your love and gift of salvation in the person of Jesus Christ.

Jesus, I believe you died on a cross and shed your blood for my sins and the sins of the whole world. I believe God raised you from the dead on the third day. Jesus, come into my heart. Take away my stony heart and give me a new heart that I may love the Father even as you do.

If you prayed this prayer, please write us or contact us at:

Covenant of Life Ministries
P.O. Box 43055
Mississauga, ON L5B 4A7
E-mail: info@covenantoflife.org
Web site: www.covenantoflife.org.

Let me pray for you:

Father, I thank you in the name of Jesus that your Spirit will witness with my brother or sister that they are children of God. Father, make known to them your ways and show them your covenant. Manifest your presence and touch them deeply with your Holy Spirit and unveil your Word to them continually. Amen.

ORDER FORM

To order more copies of *Here Comes Ishmael*, please use the order form below (please print):

Name: _____

Address: _____

City: _____ State/Prov:_____

Zip/Postal Code: _____ Telephone: _____

_____ copies @ $19.95 USD/$24.95 CAD: $_____

Shipping: ($5.00 first book – $1.00 each add. book) $_____

Total amount enclosed: $_____

Payable by Cheque or Postal Money Order

(Please make checks payable to Covenant of Life Ministries.
Allow time for checks to clear.)

Send to: *Covenant of Life Media Inc.*
P.O Box 43055
Mississauga, ON
L5B 4A7

or you can call (877) 220 3030
or visit us online at www.covenantoflife.org.